Ninja Foodi
Cookbook for Beginners
with Pictures

1200 Days Easy & Delicious Air Fry, Broil, Pressure Cook, Slow Cook, Dehydrate, and More Recipes for Beginners and Advanced Users

Janice Sottile

TABLE OF CONTENTS

Introduction..5

    What is Ninja Foodi Multi-Cooker? 5
    Main Functions of Ninja Foodi Multi-Cooker... 6
    Buttons and User Guide of Ninja Foodi Multi-Cooker.. 6
    How to Clean and Maintain 7

Breakfast Recipes 8

    Ninja Foodi Ham Muffins 8
    Ninja Foodi Baked Eggs............................ 8
    Nutmeg Pumpkin Porridge 8
    Brussels Sprouts Bacon Hash.................... 9
    Apricot Oatmeal.................................... 9
    Chicken Omelet 9
    Swiss Bacon Frittata 10
    Vanilla Banana Bread.............................10
    Ham Breakfast Casserole 11
    Almond Quinoa Porridge.........................11
    Deviled Eggs 11
    Chorizo Omelet 12
    Ninja Foodi Coconut Cereal......................12
    Pepperoni Omelets 12
    Ninja Foodi Eggs with Spinach 13
    Avocado Cups.....................................13
    Hashbrown Casserole 13
    Ninja Foodi Cinnamon Tea 14
    Breakfast pizza 14
    Ninja Foodi Broccoli Pancakes 15
    Ninja Foodi Arugula Omelet 15
    Ninja Foodi Pancakes 15
    Breakfast Oats Bowl 16
    Fruit Pancakes 16
    Ninja Foodi Hard-boiled eggs 16
    French Toast Bites 17
    Egg rolls 17

Snacks and Appetizers Recipes 18

    Cauliflower Nuggets..............................18
    Ninja Foodi Popcorn..............................18
    Glazed Walnuts 19
    Crispy Onion Rings 19
    Chicken Pork Nuggets 19
    Japanese Eggs 20
    Garlicky Tomato 20
    Shallots with Mushrooms 20
    Jalapeno Salsa....................................21
    Crispy Chicken Skin...............................21
    Ninja Foodi Spicy Popcorns 22
    Ninja Foodi Spinach Chips 22
    Ninja Foodi Cod Sticks 22
    Ninja Foodi Cheddar Biscuits....................23
    Ninja Foodi Spiced Almonds.....................23
    Zucchini Egg Tots 23
    Shallot Pepper Pancakes 24
    Ninja Foodi Spicy Peanuts 24
    Ninja Foodi Banana Cookies.....................25
    Ninja Foodi Chickpea Crackers 25

    Garlic Pretzels with Ranch Dressing 25
    Buffalo Cauliflower Platter 26
    Ninja Foodi Lemon Scones 26
    Ninja Foodi Herb Crackers 27
    Air Crisped Chicken Nuggets....................27
    Coated Onion Rings...............................27
    Ninja Foodi Spicy Cashews 28
    Chicken Wings.....................................28

Chicken and Poultry Recipes 29

    Sesame Chicken Wings 29
    Chicken Potato Stew..............................29
    Garlic turkey Breasts 30
    Lemon Chicken 30
    Chicken and Broccoli 30
    Ham-Stuffed Turkey Rolls.......................31
    Ninja Foodi Turkey & Beans Wrap 31
    Shredded Chicken Salsa.........................32
    Chicken Tortilla 32
    Paprika Chicken 32
    Ninja Foodi Lime Chicken Soup 33
    Jalapeno Chicken Nachos 33
    Ninja Foodi Chicken & Carrot Stew 34
    Ninja Foodi Turkey Stew.........................34
    Ninja Foodi Duck Stew 34
    Ninja Foodi Chicken & Salsa Chili 35
    Ninja Foodi Cranberry Chicken 35
    Ninja Foodi Ground Turkey 36
    Glazed Chicken & Vegetables...................36
    Turkey Cutlets 36
    Ninja Foodi Spinach Chicken....................37
    Ninja Foodi Chicken Broth 37
    Ninja Foodi Basil Pesto Chicken 38
    Ninja Foodi Duck Fajita Platter 38
    Ninja Foodi Barbeque Chicken Drumsticks...38
    Ninja Foodi Duck Broth 39
    Parmesan Chicken................................39
    Chicken Vegetable Soup.........................40
    Pulled Barbecue Chicken 40
    Honey Garlic Chicken............................41
    Mexican Chicken with Rice 41

Beef, Pork and Lamb Recipes 42

    Maple Glazed Pork Chops 42
    Rosemary Lamb Chops 42
    Beef Sirloin Steak 42
    Ninja Foodi Pork Shoulder Roast 43
    Ninja Foodi Carrot & Pork Stew 43
    Ninja Foodi Beef Casserole 43
    Corned Beef 44
    Korean Ribs..44
    Beef Bourguignon 44
    Cheesy Beef Casserole..........................45
    Veggies & Beef Stew 45
    Carne Guisada....................................46
    Beef Lasagna......................................46
    Braised Lamb Shanks 46

Beef Prime Roast................................47
Sweet and Sour Pork 47
Ninja Foodi Lamb & Kale Stew 48
Ninja Foodi Beef Chili.........................48
Ninja Foodi Lamb & Carrot Stew................48
Ninja Foodi Lamb Chops with Tomatoes 49
Ninja Foodi Plum & Beef Salad 49
Ninja Foodi Filling Beef Dish 49
Ninja Foodi Minced Beef with Tomatoes.......50
Ninja Foodi Ground Beef Soup 50
Ninja Foodi Steak Fajitas.......................50
Ninja Foodi Spinach Beef Soup..................51
Tomahawk Rib-Eye Steak 51
Beef Onion Pattie Burgers 52
Roasted Beef 52
Char Siu Pork 52
Beef Stew 53
Lamb Shanks...................................53
Maple Lamb Chops 54
Pork Tenderloin 54

Fish and Seafood Recipes....................... 55

Sweet Sour Fish...............................55
Cajun Shrimp 55
Panko Crusted Cod............................55
Buttery Scallops................................56
Ninja Foodi Salmon Soup 56
Salmon Kale Meal..............................56
Ninja Foodi Squid Rings 57
Ninja Foodi Stir-Fried Shrimp..................57
Ninja Foodi Rosemary Scallops.................57
Ninja Foodi Parsley Baked Salmon 58
Ninja Foodi Broiled Mahi-Mahi...................58
Ninja Foodi Roasted Tilapia.......................58
Ninja Foodi Salmon 59
Instant Catfish Fillet 59
Ninja Foodi Air Crisp Herbed Salmon 59
Ninja Foodi Ginger Cod 60
Spicy Shrimps 60
Ninja Foodi Salmon with Sweet Potatoes 60
Mixed Seafood Platter..........................61
Beer Battered Fish.............................61
Gluten-free fish tacos 62
Lobster Tail....................................62
Fish Skewers 63
Crumbed Tilapia................................63
Lemon Garlic Scallops.........................63
Ninja Foodi Asparagus Scallops 64
Ninja Foodi Ginger Salmon 64

Vegetables Recipes 65

Hawaiian Fried Rice 65
Ninja Foodi Cauliflower Fried Rice..............65
Cauliflower chunks with Lemon Sauce........66
Radish Apples Salad 66
Balsamic Cabbage with Endives 66
Veggie Pot Pie.................................67
Air Crisped Brussels Sprouts...................67
Maple Dipped Kale.............................68

Ninja Foodi Spinach and Onion Soup 68
Ninja Foodi Asparagus Soup 68
Ninja Foodi Broccoli Soup.......................69
Ninja Foodi Vegetables Smoothie 69
Cabbage with Bacon...........................69
Cabbage with Carrots 70
Saucy Kale.....................................70
Bell Peppers Mix 70
Ninja Foodi Tomato Olive Salad.................71
Ninja Foodi Roasted Red Pepper Gazpacho ..71
Ninja Foodi Kale Salad 71
Minty Radishes 72
Beets and Carrots 72
Steak and Veggie Bowl 72
Sesame Radish 73
Kale and Parmesan............................73
Carrots Walnuts Salad 73
Ninja Foodi Vegetable Curry 74
Ninja Foodi Citrus Carrots 74
Gluten-free Taco Beans 74
Pomegranate Radish Mix 75
Broccoli Cauliflower 75
Leeks and Carrots 75

Dessert Recipes 76

Vanilla Cheesecake............................76
Yogurt Cheesecake............................76
Chocolate Cheesecake 77
Mini Chocolate Cheesecakes 77
Lime Blueberry Cheesecake....................78
Chocolate Walnut Cake 78
Ninja Foodi Vanilla Shake 79
Ninja Foodi Mocha Cake 79
Ninja Foodi Chia Seed Smoothie 79
Ninja Foodi Fruity Frozen Treat 80
Ninja Foodi Ricotta Mousse......................80
Ninja Foodi Chickpea Fudge....................80
Ninja Foodi Blackberry Crumble 81
Ninja Foodi Yogurt Cheesecake 81
Ninja Foodi Banana Custard 82
Ninja Foodi Chocolate Tofu Mousse............82
Ninja Foodi Raspberry Ice Cream 82
Rocky Road Fudge.............................83
Biscuit Donuts 83
Pineapple Chunks..............................84
Banana Bread..................................84
Honey Almond Scones 84
Chocolate Chip Cookies........................85
Mini Vanilla Cheesecakes.......................85

4 Weeks Meal Plan 86

Week 1 86
Week 2 86
Week 3 87
Week 4 87

Conclusion 88

Appendix Measurement Conversion Chart89

What is Ninja Foodi Multi-Cooker?

The Ninja Foodi Multi-Cooker is the ultimate Pressure Cook, transforming even the toughest ingredients into tender, juicy, and flavorful meals in less time than you could have imagined. And, thanks to the powerful crisping lid, the Ninja Foodi Multi-Cooker is also the ultimate Air Crisp, allowing you to indulge in your favorite fried foods guilt-free.

Enjoy them separately or combine them to turn your food into a tender crisp. Its innovative crisping lid allows you to air fry, bake/roast, and broil, allowing you to pressure cook to seal in juices and finish with a crisp.

The Ninja Foodi Multi-Cooker uses super-heated steam to quickly infuse moisture and flavor into pressure cooked foods, then the powerful crisping lid unleashes rapid-hot air down and back all around your food for a crispy, golden finish that other Pressure Cooks can only dream of. The result is a finished dish that is far more than just done, and it will allow anyone – even those short on time – to make it.

The Ninja Foodi Multi-Cooker differs from other Pressure Cooks in terms of crisp clear results.

Foods can be transformed from frozen to crispy using the following methods: Have you forgotten to thaw tonight's dinner? Procrastinators are overjoyed. Frozen meats like steak or even two pounds of chicken wings can be transformed into crispy meals in as little as 30 minutes! Pressure cooking allows you to defrost and tenderize food at the same time. Then, to give your meals a crispy finish, remove the crisping lid.

Variety of Meals: Prepare full meals with main dishes and sides like proteins, veggies, and grains all in one pot – each with its own distinct, flavorful texture.

Feed the Whole Family: The Ninja Foodi Multi-6.5-quart Cooker's cooking pot can hold a six-pound roast. The 4-quart Cook & Air Crisp basket can also be used to cook three pounds of French fries, two pounds of chicken wings, or even a five-pound chicken.

Simple Cleanup: With only one nonstick, ceramic-coated pot to clean after cooking, saves time.

Main Functions of Ninja Foodi Multi-Cooker

1. Pressure Cook
2. Air Fryer
3. Air Crisp
4. Slow Cooker
5. Steamer
6. Sear/Sauté
7. Bake/Roast
8. Broiler
9. Dehydrate

Air Crisp

Cook under pressure to seal in the juices and crisp for the perfect finish. To add a delicious golden crunch to your food, switch from the Pressure Lid to the Crisping Lid.

Perfectly crispy chips, golden vegetable crisps, and guilt-free fried food are available. Traditional frying methods use up to 75% less fat. With little to no oil, you can enjoy crispy fries, golden vegetable crisps, and guilt-free fried food. Deep-fried, hand-cut French fries were put to the test.

Pressure Cook

Traditional cooking methods are up to 70% faster. Advanced security features provide you with peace of mind. Meals ready in minutes. Superheated steam cooks steak and roast chicken quickly, as well as chili and one-pot meals, delectable desserts, and more.

Slow Cooker

Ensure your meal is ready when you get home. From tender pulled pork to casserole and risotto.

Cook both the main course and the sides at the same time. Using the reversible rack, layer vegetables and grains with meat, fish, or proteins for quick, one-pot meals. With variable temperature settings and a variety of cooking functions, you can precisely ROAST, GRILL, STEAM, SAUTÉ, BAKE, and more. Dinner will be ready whenever you are. Adjust the HIGH time setting to any time between four and 12 hours, or cook on LOW for six to 12 hours.

Buttons and User Guide of Ninja Foodi Multi-Cooker

- **Pressure Cook Button**: Settings for Hi and Low pressure.

- **Steam Button:** There is no temperature adjustment. You can set the timer to up to 30 minutes. When using this feature, make sure the black valve on the top is set to vent rather than seal.

- **Slow Cook Button**: control with adjustable time settings and High and Low cooking temperatures.

- **Air Crisp Button:** Temperature settings from 300° F to 400° F.

- **Sear/Sauté:** This feature has several temperature settings, including Hi, Med-Hi, Med, Med-Low, and Low. This feature does not allow you to configure the time. It will remain turned on until you turn it off.

- **Bake/Roast:** The Bake/Roast feature has temperature settings ranging from 250° F to 400° F, and the time can be set to up to four hours.

- **Broil:** There is no temperature adjustment for the Broil Function; it is either on or off. You can set the timer to up to 30 minutes.

- **Multi-Purpose Pan:** Dimension: 8.7 inches D and 2.5 inches H

You can make bubbly casseroles, sweets or any bake products by using this pan in your Ninja Foodi Multi-Cooker.

- **Crisper Pan:** Dimension: 9 inches D and 0.75-inch H

This pan is perforated with holes so you can use this pan to make crisping pizza or vegetables or also to reheat any item.

- **Loaf Pan:** Dimension: 8.25" × 4.25" × 3.5"

Perfect pan for baking bread and other items in your Ninja Foodi Multi-Cooker.

How to Clean and Maintain

1. The unit should be cleaned thoroughly after every use.

2. Before cleaning, unplug the unit from the outlet.

3. **Never** put the cooker base in the dishwasher or submerge it in water or other liquid.

4. Wipe the cooker base and control panel clean with a clean damp cloth.

5. The dishwasher is safe for the cooking pot, silicone ring, reversible rack, Cook & Crisp Basket, and detachable diffuser.

6. Water and dish soap can be used to clean the pressure lid, including the pressure release valve and anti-clog cap. **Do not** use the dishwasher to clean the pressure lid or any of its components, and **do not** disassemble the pressure release valve or red float valve assembly.

7. After the heat shield has cooled, wipe down the crisping lid with a wet cloth or paper towel.

8. If there is food residue on the cooking pot, reversible rack, or Cook & Crisp Basket, fill it with water and soak it before cleaning. **Scouring pads should not be used**. Scrub with a non-abrasive cleanser or liquid dish soap and a nylon pad or brush if necessary.

9. After each use, air-dry all parts or use a soft dry towel.

Ninja Foodi Ham Muffins

Prep Time: 10 minutes
Cook Time: 20 minutes
Servings: 4

Ingredients:
- 4 eggs
- ½ cup cooked ham, crumbled
- ½ cup red bell pepper, seeded and chopped
- 1 tablespoon water
- Salt and black pepper, to taste

Directions:
1. Add eggs, salt, pepper and water in a bowl. Mix well.
2. Now, add in red bell pepper and crumbled ham. Mix well and set aside.
3. Pour the mixture in greased muffin-tins and place them in the pot of Ninja Foodi Multi-cooker.
4. Select "Bake" and close the Crisping Lid.
5. Press the "Start/Stop" button and bake for 20 minutes at 350 degrees F.
6. Take out, serve and enjoy!

Nutritional Values Per Serving:
Calories: 95; Fat: 5.9g; Carbohydrates: 2.1g; Protein: 8.5g

Ninja Foodi Baked Eggs

Prep Time: 12 minutes
Cook Time: 9 minutes
Servings: 3

Ingredients:
- 3 eggs
- 3 tablespoons low-fat parmesan cheese, shredded
- ½ cup fresh spinach, chopped finely
- 3 tablespoons heavy cream
- 3 tablespoons olive oil
- Salt and black pepper, to taste

Directions:
1. Grease three muffin tins with olive oil and add spinach in them.
2. Add in eggs and top them with heavy cream, parmesan cheese, salt and pepper.
3. Place the muffin tins in the pot of Ninja Foodi Multi-cooker and select "Bake".
4. Close the Crisping Lid and press the "Start/Stop" button.
5. Bake for 9 minutes at 400 degrees F and open the lid.
6. Take out, serve and enjoy!

Nutritional Values Per Serving:
Calories: 326; Fat: 29.9g; Carbohydrates: 2g; Protein: 15g

Nutmeg Pumpkin Porridge

Prep Time: 15 minutes
Cook Time: 5 hours
Servings: 8

Ingredients:
- 1 cup unsweetened almond milk
- 2 pounds pumpkin, peeled and cubed into ½-inch size
- 6-8 drops liquid stevia
- ½ teaspoon ground allspice
- 1 tablespoon ground cinnamon
- 1 teaspoon ground nutmeg
- ¼ teaspoon ground cloves
- ½ cup walnuts, chopped

Directions:
1. In the Ninja Foodi's insert, place ½ cup of almond milk and remaining ingredients and stir to combine.
2. Close the Ninja Foodi's lid with a crisping lid and select "Slow Cook".
3. Set on "LO" for 4-5 hours.
4. Press the "Start/Stop" button to initiate cooking.

5. Open the Ninja Foodi's lid and stir in the remaining almond milk.
6. With a potato masher, mash the mixture completely.
7. Divide the porridge into serving bowls evenly.
8. Serve warm with the topping of walnuts.

Nutritional Values Per Serving:
Calories: 96; Fat: 5.5g; Carbohydrates: 11.2g; Protein: 3.3g

Brussels Sprouts Bacon Hash

Prep Time: 10 minutes
Cook Time: 20 minutes
Servings: 4

Ingredients:
- ½ lb. brussels sprouts, sliced in half
- 4 slices bacon, chopped
- ½ red onion, chopped
- salt, to taste
- black pepper, to taste

Directions:
1. Toss all the ingredients into the Ninja Foodi cooking pot.
2. Secure the Ninja Foodi lid and turn its pressure handle to 'SEAL' position.
3. Select mode for 20 minutes at HI.
4. Once done, release the steam naturally then remove the lid.
5. Serve fresh.

Nutritional Values Per Serving:
Calories 121; Total Fat 9 g; Total Carbs 13.8 g; Protein 4.3 g

Apricot Oatmeal

Prep Time: 10 minutes
Cook Time: 8 hours
Servings: 8

Ingredients:
- 2 cups steel-cut oats
- ⅓ cup dried apricots, chopped
- ½ cup dried cherries
- 1 teaspoon ground cinnamon
- 4 cups milk
- 4 cups water
- ¼ teaspoon liquid stevia

Directions:
1. In the Ninja Foodi's insert, place all ingredients and stir to combine.
2. Close the Ninja Foodi's lid with a pressure lid and select "Slow Cook."
3. Set on "LO" for 6-8 hours.
4. Press the "Start/Stop" button to initiate cooking.
5. Open the Ninja Foodi's lid and serve warm.

Nutritional Values Per Serving:
Calories: 148; Fat: 3.5g; Carbohydrates: 4.2 g; Protein: 5.9 g

Chicken Omelet

Prep Time: 10 minutes
Cook Time: 16 minutes
Servings: 2

Ingredients:
- 1 teaspoon butter
- 1 small yellow onion, chopped
- ½ jalapeño pepper, seeded and chopped
- 3 eggs
- Black pepper and salt, as required
- ¼ cup cooked chicken, shredded

Directions:
1. Select the "Sauté/Sear" setting of Ninja Foodi and place the butter into the pot.
2. Press the "Start/Stop" button to initiate cooking and heat for about 2-3 minutes.
3. Add the onion and cook for about 4-5 minutes.
4. Add the jalapeño pepper and cook for about 1 minute.

5. Meanwhile, in a suitable, add the eggs, salt, and black pepper and beat well.
6. Press the "Start/Stop" button to pause cooking and stir in the chicken.
7. Top with the egg mixture evenly.
8. Close the Ninja Foodi's lid with a crisping lid and select "Air Crisp."
9. Set its cooking temperature to 355 degrees F for 5 minutes.
10. Press the "Start/Stop" button to initiate cooking.
11. Open the Ninja Foodi's lid and transfer the omelette onto a plate.
12. Cut into equal-sized wedges and serve hot.

Nutritional Values Per Serving:
Calories: 153; Fat: 9.1g; Carbohydrates: 4g; Protein: 13.8g

Swiss Bacon Frittata

Prep Time: 10 minutes
Cook Time: 23 minutes
Servings: 6

Ingredients:
- 1 small onion, chopped
- ½ lb. of raw bacon, chopped
- 1 lb. of frozen spinach
- 10 eggs
- 1 cup cottage cheese
- ½ cup half and half cream
- 1 tsp salt
- 1 cup shredded swiss cheese

Directions:
1. Preheat your Ninja Foodi for 5 minutes at MD:HI on Sear/Sauté Mode.
2. Add bacon, and onion to the Foodi and sauté for 10 minutes until crispy.
3. Stir in spinach and stir cook for 3 minutes.
4. Whisk eggs with cottage cheese, salt and half and half cream in a bowl.
5. Pour this mixture into the Ninja Foodi cooking pot.
6. Drizzle swiss cheese over the egg mixture.
7. Secure the Ninja Foodi lid and switch the Foodi to Bake/Roast mode for 20 minutes at 350

degrees F.
8. Serve warm.

Nutritional Values Per Serving:
Calories 139; Total Fat 10.1g; Total Carbs 2.3g; Protein 10.1g

Vanilla Banana Bread

Prep Time: 10 minutes
Cook Time: 50 minutes
Servings: 8

Ingredients:
- 2 cups flour
- 1 teaspoon baking powder
- ½ cup erythritol
- ½ cup butter softened
- 2 eggs
- 1 tablespoon vanilla extract
- 4 bananas, peeled and mashed

Directions:
1. Grease a 7-inch springform pan.
2. In a suitable, mix flour and baking powder.
3. In another bowl, add erythritol, butter, and eggs and beat until creamy.
4. Add the bananas and vanilla extract and beat until well combined.
5. Slowly add flour mixture, 1 cup at a time, and mix until smooth.
6. Place mixture into prepared loaf pan evenly.
7. In the Ninja Foodi's insert, place 1 cup of water.
8. Set the "Reversible Rack" in the Ninja Foodi's insert.
9. Place the pan over the "Reversible Rack."
10. Close the Ninja Foodi's lid with the pressure lid and place the pressure valve to the "Seal" position.
11. Select "Pressure" mode and set it to "High" for 50 minutes.
12. Press the "Start/Stop" button to initiate cooking.
13. Switch the pressure valve to "Vent" and do a "Quick" release.
14. Cut into desired sized slices and serve.

Nutritional Values Per Serving:
Calories: 336; Fat: 13.1 g; Carbohydrates: 50.4 g; Protein: 5.4g

Ham Breakfast Casserole

Prep Time: 10 minutes
Cook Time: 10 minutes
Servings: 4

Ingredients:
- 4 whole eggs
- 1 tablespoons milk
- 1 cup ham, cooked and chopped
- ½ cup cheddar cheese, shredded
- ¼ teaspoon salt
- ¼ teaspoon black pepper

Directions:
1. Take a baking pan small enough to fit into your Ninja Foodi bowl, and grease it well with butter
2. Take a medium bowl and whisk in eggs, milk, salt, pepper and add ham, cheese, and stir
3. Pour mixture into baking pan and lower the pan into your Ninja Foodi
4. Set your Ninja Foodi Air Crisp mode and Air Crisp for 325 degrees F for 7 minutes
5. Remove pan from eggs and enjoy.

Nutritional Values Per Serving:
Calories: 169; Fat: 13g; Carbohydrates: 1g; Protein: 12g

Almond Quinoa Porridge

Prep Time: 10 minutes
Cook Time: 1 minute
Servings: 6

Ingredients:
- 1¼ cups water
- 1 cup almond milk
- 1½ cups uncooked quinoa, rinsed
- 1 tablespoon choc zero maple syrup
- 1 cinnamon stick

- Pinch of salt

Directions:
1. In the Ninja Foodi's insert, add all ingredients and stir to combine well.
2. Close the Ninja Foodi's pressure lid and place the pressure valve in the "Seal" position.
3. Select "Pressure" mode and set it to "Hi" for 1 minute.
4. Press the "Start/Stop" button to initiate cooking.
5. Now turn the pressure valve to "Vent" and do a "Quick" release.
6. Open the Ninja Foodi's lid, and with a fork, fluff the quinoa.
7. Serve warm.

Nutritional Values Per Serving:
Calories: 186; Fat: 2.6 g; Carbohydrates: 4.8 g; Protein: 6 g

Deviled Eggs

Prep Time: 10 minutes
Cook Time: 10 minutes
Servings: 4

Ingredients:
- 8 large eggs
- 1 cup of water
- Guacamole
- Sliced Radishes
- Mayonnaise
- Furikake

Directions:
1. Add water to the inner insert of your Ninja Foodi.
2. Place the steamer rack inside the pot and set the eggs on top of the rack.
3. Lock pressure lid and cook on "HIGH" pressure for 6 minutes.
4. Release Pressure naturally over 10 minutes and transfer the eggs to a suitable full of icy water.
5. Peel after 5 minutes.
6. Cut in half and decorate with guacamole, sliced radish, mayo and enjoy.

Nutritional Values Per Serving:
Calories: 70; Fat: 6g; Carbohydrates: 1g; Protein: 3g

Chorizo Omelet

Prep Time: 10 minutes
Cook Time: 30-35 minutes
Servings: 4

Ingredients:
- 3 eggs, whisked
- 3 ounces chorizo, chopped
- 1-ounce Feta cheese, crumbled
- 5 tablespoons almond milk
- ¾ teaspoon chilli flakes
- ¼ teaspoon salt
- 1 green pepper, chopped

Directions:
1. Add listed ingredients to a suitable and mix well.
2. Take an omelette pan and pour the mixture on it.
3. Pre-heat your Ninja Food on "BAKE/ROAST" mode at a temperature of 320 degrees F.
4. Transfer pan with omelette mix to your Ninja Foodi and cook for 30 minutes, or until the surface is golden and the egg has set properly
5. Serve and enjoy.

Nutritional Values Per Serving:
Calories: 426; Fat: 38g; Carbohydrates: 7g; Protein: 21g

Ninja Foodi Coconut Cereal

Prep Time: 5 minutes
Cook Time: 8 hours 3 minutes
Servings: 3

Ingredients:
- ½ cup unsweetened coconut, shredded

- 1 cup water
- ¼ teaspoon ground cinnamon
- ⅛ teaspoon liquid stevia
- 1 cup unsweetened almond milk
- ¼ cup coconut flour, divided
- ¼ teaspoon vanilla extract

Directions:
1. Add shredded coconut, almond milk, half of the coconut flour, water and cinnamon in the pot of Ninja Foodi. Mix well.
2. Close the pressure Lid and select "Slow Cook".
3. Set on LOW TEMP for 8 hours and press the "Start/Stop" button.
4. Open the lid and add in the remaining coconut flour, stevia and vanilla extract. Mix until well combined.
5. Close the pressure Lid and cook for 3 minutes.
6. Open the lid and take out.
7. Serve and enjoy!

Nutritional Values Per Serving:
Calories: 102; Fat: 6.6g; Carbohydrates: 9.6g; Protein: 2.1g

Pepperoni Omelets

Prep Time: 10 minutes
Cook Time: 5 minutes
Servings: 4

Ingredients:
- 4 tablespoons heavy cream
- 15 pepperoni slices
- 2 tablespoons butter
- Black pepper and salt to taste
- 6 whole eggs

Directions:
1. Take a suitable and whisk in eggs, cream, pepperoni slices, salt, and pepper.
2. Set your Ninja Foodi to "Sear/Sauté" mode and add butter and egg mix.
3. Sauté for 3 minutes, flip.
4. Lock and secure the Ninja Foodi's crisping lid and Air Crisp for 2 minutes at 350 degrees F
5. Transfer to a serving plate and enjoy.

Nutritional Values Per Serving:
Calories: 141; Fat: 11g; Carbohydrates: 0.6g; Protein: 9g

Ninja Foodi Eggs with Spinach

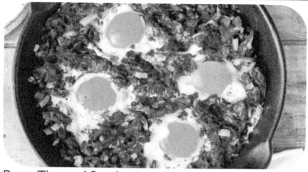

Prep Time: 10 minutes
Cook Time: 25 minutes
Servings: 4

Ingredients:
- 2 tablespoons olive oil
- 4 eggs
- ¼ cup scallion, chopped
- 10 cups chopped baby spinach
- Salt and black pepper, to taste

Directions:
1. Add oil and scallion in the pot of Ninja Foodi Multi-cooker and cook for 5 minutes with an open lid.
2. Add in pepper, salt and spinach and cook for 5-minutes.
3. Make fourwells in the mixture and crack eggs in each well.
4. Close the Crisping Lid and select "Bake".
5. Press the "Start/Stop" button and bake for 15 minutes at 400 degrees F.
6. Take out, serve and enjoy!

Nutritional Values Per Serving:
Calories: 142; Fat: 11.7g; Carbohydrates: 3.5g; Protein: 7.8g

Avocado Cups

Prep Time: 10 minutes
Cook Time: 12 minutes
Servings: 2

Ingredients:
- 1 avocado, halved and pitted
- Black pepper and salt, as required
- 2 eggs
- 1 tablespoon Parmesan cheese, shredded
- 1 teaspoon fresh chives, minced

Directions:
1. Set a greased square piece of foil in "Air Crisp Basket."
2. Set the "Air Crisp Basket" in the Ninja Foodi's insert.
3. Close the Ninja Foodi's lid with a crisping lid and select "Bake/Roast".
4. Set its cooking temperature to 390 degrees F for 5 minutes.
5. Press the "Start/Stop" button to initiate pre-heating.
6. Carefully scoop out about 2 teaspoons of flesh from each avocado half.
7. Crack 1 egg in each avocado half and sprinkle with salt, black pepper, and cheese.
8. After preheating, Open the Ninja Foodi's lid.
9. Place the avocado halves into the "Air Crisp Basket."
10. Close the Ninja Foodi's lid with a crisping lid and Select "Bake/Roast."
11. Set its cooking temperature to 390 degrees F for about 12 minutes.
12. Press the "Start/Stop" button to initiate cooking.
13. Open the Ninja Foodi's lid and transfer the avocado halves onto serving plates.
14. Top with Parmesan and chives and serve.

Nutritional Values Per Serving:
Calories: 278; Fat: 24.7g; Carbohydrates: 9.1g; Protein: 8.4g

Hashbrown Casserole

Prep Time: 10 Minutes
Cook Time: 20 Minutes
Servings: 6

Ingredients:
- 6 eggs
- 30 ounce bag frozen hash browns
- ¼ cup milk
- 1 tablespoon pizza sauce
- 2 tablespoons olive oil
- 1 medium-sized onion (chopped)
- 1 pound ham
- ½ cup cheddar cheese

Directions:
1. Turn on the Air Crisp Mode at Medium temperature on your Ninja Foodi Multi-Cooker.
2. Add chopped onions and olive oil. Cook it till the color becomes translucent.
3. Add pizza sauce for that pop of flavor.
4. Then add the frozen hash browns to it. Add eggs on the hash browns.
5. Add the meat to the top of the pot.
6. Place Ninja Foodi Multi-Cooker on Air Crisp Mode at 390° F for 10 minutes at least, or wait until the top turns golden brown and the eggs are done.
7. Add cheddar cheese on top, close the lid and let the cheddar cheese melt for about 1 minute!

Nutritional Values Per Serving:
Calories: 682; Fat: 8g; Carbohydrates: 5g; Protein: 16g

Ninja Foodi Cinnamon Tea

Prep Time: 5 minutes
Cook Time: 12 minutes
Servings: 2

Ingredients:
- 1 cup water
- 1 teaspoon black tea
- 2 cinnamon sticks
- 4 black peppercorns
- ½ cup fat-free cream

Directions:
1. Add water, peppercorns and cinnamon in the pot Ninja Foodi Multi-cooker.
2. Boil for about 10 minutes and add in cream.
3. Close the pressure Lid and select "Pressure".
4. Press the "Start/Stop" button and cook for about 2 minutes at LOW pressure.
5. Open the lid and strain the tea.
6. Serve hot and enjoy!

Nutritional Values Per Serving:
Calories: 62; Fat: 0.8g; Carbohydrates: 5.4g; Protein: 8.5g

Breakfast pizza

Prep Time: 10 Minutes
Cook Time: 20 Minutes
Servings: 4

Ingredients:
For the Pizza Dough:
- 100 grams all-purpose flour
- 1 tablespoon sugar (granulated)
- 1 teaspoon baking powder
- ¼ teaspoon table salt
- Greek yogurt ⅔ cup

For Topping Purposes:
- ¾ slices of center cut bacon
- 4 beaten eggs
- 3 ounces cheddar/ mozzarella cheese (freshly cut)

Directions:
1. Mix all the dry ingredients including flour, baking powder, and salt in a container. Do this before adding the yogurt. Mix everything up with a spatula until crumbly. Now form a ball of the dough onto the flat surface.
2. Create a thicker edge for the crust than in the center. The diameter of the dough should be around 8. A rolling pin could be used as a good option here.
3. Give a Cook & Crisp Basket the oil spray before adding the crust. Brush a bit more cooking spray.
4. For 10 minutes start Air Crisp Mode at 390° F before flipping. Air Crisp for an additional 3 minutes at 390° F before adding the toppings.
5. While the crust is being cooked, over medium-high heat adds bacon strips to a non-stick skillet. Remove the skillet from the heat once fully cooked and then add eggs.
6. Stir to scramble the eggs and then add cream cheese once eggs are nearly fully done.
7. Now add the bacon and egg mixture to the crust. Top with cheddar cheese and let it melt completely for three to 4 minutes. After that, the pizza is done and you can enjoy it!

Nutritional Values Per Serving:
Calories: 313; Fat: 7g; Carbohydrates: 12g; Protein: 19g

Ninja Foodi Broccoli Pancakes

Prep Time: 5 minutes
Cook Time: 20 minutes
Servings: 2

Ingredients:
- ¼ cup chopped broccoli
- ¼ cup low-fat cheddar cheese, shredded
- ½ teaspoon dried onion, minced
- 1 egg
- ½ teaspoon garlic powder
- Salt and black pepper, to taste

Directions:
1. Add everything in a food-processor and pulse until a smooth mixture is formed.
2. Pour the mixture in the pot of Ninja Foodi Multi-cooker and select "Bake".
3. Close the Crisping Lid and press the "Start/Stop" button.
4. Bake for about 20 minutes at 400 degrees F and open the lid.
5. Take out and serve hot.

Nutritional Values Per Serving:
Calories: 95; Fat: 6.9g; Carbohydrates: 1.7g; Protein: 6.8g

Ninja Foodi Arugula Omelet

Prep Time: 10 minutes
Cook Time: 5 minutes
Servings: 4

Ingredients:
- 6 eggs
- 2 tablespoons unsweetened almond milk
- 2 cups fresh arugula, chopped
- 4 scallion, chopped finely
- 2 tablespoons olive oil
- Salt and black pepper, to taste

Directions:
1. Add everything except olive oil in a bowl. Whisk well.
2. Now, heat olive oil in the pot of Ninja Foodi Multi-cooker and add in egg mixture.
3. Press the "Steam" button and close the pressure Lid.
4. Press the "Start/Stop" button and cook for about 5-minutes on low heat.
5. Open the pressure Lid and take out.
6. Serve and enjoy!

Nutritional Values Per Serving:
Calories: 163; Fat: 13.8g; Carbohydrates: 2.1g; Protein: 8.9g

Ninja Foodi Pancakes

Prep Time: 10 minutes
Cook Time: 25 minutes
Servings: 2

Ingredients:
- ¼ cup fat-free milk
- ½ tablespoon canola oil
- ¼ teaspoon ground nutmeg
- ¼ cup all-purpose flour
- 1 egg
- 2 tablespoons sugar

Directions:
1. Add milk, ground nutmeg, all-purpose flour, egg and sugar in a large bowl. Whisk properly.
2. Pour egg mixture in the pot of Ninja Foodi Multi-cooker and close the Crisping Lid.
3. Select "Bake" and press the "Start/Stop" button.
4. Bake for 20 minutes at 400 degrees F and open the Crisping Lid.
5. Take out, serve and enjoy!

Nutritional Values Per Serving:
Calories: 177; Fat: 5.9g; Carbohydrates: 25.7g; Protein: 5.4g

Breakfast Oats Bowl

Prep Time: 3 Minutes
Cook Time: 8 Minutes
Servings: 2

Ingredients:
- 1 cup oats
- 1.5 cup milk
- 1.5 teaspoon ground cinnamon powder
- Water as required

Optional Toppings:
- Flax seeds
- Honey
- Granola mix

Directions:
1. Add all the ingredients in the Ninja Foodi Multi-Cooker Pot.
2. Oats should be fully submerged in water. Secure the pressure lid and turn the valve to Seal. Set the Ninja Foodi Multi-Cooker to High Pressure for 5 minutes.
3. After 5 minutes turn the valve off and let the oats sit for about 5 minutes after being fully cooked and all pressure to release.
4. Serve with your favorite toppings!

Nutritional Values Per Serving:
Calories: 162; Fat: 4.8g; Carbohydrates: 12g; Protein: 9.3g

Fruit Pancakes

Prep Time: 7 Minutes
Cook Time: 20 Minutes
Servings: 2

Ingredients:
- ½ cup of pancake mix oats
- 2 eggs
- ¼ cup regular milk
- 1 teaspoon melted butter
- 2 drops of Vanilla essence
- 1 date
- ½ teaspoon cinnamon
- ½ cup of any fresh fruit of your choice

Directions:
1. In a mixing bowl mix together the pancake mix or oats, eggs, melted butter, cinnamon, dates, vanilla essence, and milk until a thick batter is prepared.
2. Gently mix in available fresh fruit, it can also be any thawed fruit.
3. Spray the Ninja Foodi Multi-Cooker's cooking pot with spray oil. Non-sticky canola spray could also be the best option.
4. Preheat your Ninja Foodi Multi-Cooker to 375° F on the Bake option.
5. After that, pour in the batter and it should be spread with even consistency throughout the Ninja Foodi Multi-Cooker.
6. Close the crisping lid of the Ninja Foodi Multi-Cooker and set the time of cooking to 12 to 15 minutes. 15 minutes are considered ideal for a perfect turnout of the pancake.
7. Lastly, serve it with any fruit or toppings of your choice.

Nutritional Values Per Serving:
Calories: 227.5; Fat: 8.5g; Carbohydrates: 18.5 g; Protein: 10.5 g

Ninja Foodi Hard-boiled eggs

Prep Time: 8-10 Minutes
Cook Time: 15 Minutes
Servings: 6

Ingredients:
- 12 eggs
- 1 cup water

Directions:
1. Place the Multi-purpose pan filled with one cup of water inside Ninja Foodi Multi-Cooker.
2. Be very careful while placing the eggs in the Ninja Foodi Multi-Cooker.
3. Secure the pressure lid and turn the valve to Seal. Set the Ninja Foodi Multi-Cooker to High Pressure for 5 minutes. Press START/STOP.

4. While the eggs are being done, take a bowl, add ice cubes and water.
5. After 5 minutes, turn valve for Quick Pressure Release. Then take eggs out.
6. After taking out the eggs, put them in that ice bath for 5 minutes at least.
7. Peel and serve, the eggs are ready. They can also be stored in the fridge for up to a week!

Nutritional Values Per Serving:
Calories: 155; Fat: 11g; Carbohydrates: 1g; Protein: 6g

French Toast Bites

Prep Time: 10 Minutes
Cook Time: 15 Minutes
Servings: 1

Ingredients:
- ¼ loaf of French bread
- 2 eggs
- 2 tablespoons milk
- ½ teaspoon cinnamon
- 1 mashed banana

Topping
- 1 tablespoon brown sugar
- 1 tablespoon honey
- ½ teaspoon cinnamon

Directions:
1. Cut the French bread into cubes and add it to a container.
2. In a separate small bowl, combine eggs, milk, mashed banana, vanilla, and cinnamon.
3. Pour mixture over the bread cubes and mix it all well till it's equally coated.
4. In a greased Ninja Foodi Multi-Cooker Basket, add bread pieces in a single layer.
5. Sprinkle brown sugar and cinnamon on top of it.
6. Then select Air Crisp at 390° F for 10 minutes. Keep tossing or mixing halfway through.
7. When the golden-brown color appears, drizzle the honey, bites are ready to be served!

Nutritional Values Per Serving:
Calories: 302; Fat: 6g; Carbohydrates: 21g; Protein: 13g

Egg rolls

Prep Time: 5 Minutes
Cook Time: 20 Minutes
Servings: 4

Ingredients:
- 2 teaspoons olive oil
- ½ cup chopped sliced cabbage
- 1 small carrot (thinly sliced)
- 1.5 cup boiled and shredded chicken
- 1.5 tablespoon vinegar
- 1.5 tablespoon soy sauce
- 1 tablespoon grounded herbs
- Ginger garlic as required

For the sauce:
- 1 tablespoon mustard sauce
- 1 tablespoon chili garlic sauce
- 1.5 tablespoon vinegar
- 1.5 tablespoon soy sauce

For Egg Roll Making:
- 4 wrappers
- 1 beaten egg
- 1 tablespoon olive oil/ sesame oil

Directions:
1. Slice up the vegetables; carrots and cabbage. The frozen vegetable mix could also be used here. The quantity should be about three to four cups to make four egg rolls.
2. Peel ginger garlic and grate it.
3. Now turn on the Roast function of Ninja Foodi Multi-Cooker and set the temperature on High. Add in the cabbage mix and olive oil. Add the shredded chicken.
4. After that, add in vinegar, soy sauce, ginger, and garlic paste. Stir it and steam in Ninja Foodi Multi-Cooker for three to 5 minutes or until you get your desired texture.
5. Remove the pot from heat and let it cool for a bit.
6. In Ninja Foodi Multi-Cooker for 5 minutes on Air Crisp Mode at the temperature of 390° F add the filling into an egg roll wrapper, brush its edges, and roll. Brush lightly with oil and place it on a rack in a high position in Ninja Foodi Multi-Cooker.
7. Air Crisp it for a period of ten to 15 minutes, keep flipping it every three seconds to ensure its crispiness.
8. Remove it after it's done and serve it with the dipping sauce!

Nutritional Values Per Serving:
Calories: 286; Fat: 9.5g; Carbohydrates: 16g; Protein: 22g

Cauliflower Nuggets

Prep Time: 10 minutes
Cook Time: 10 minutes
Servings: 8

Ingredients:
- 8 ounces cauliflower
- 1 big red onion, chopped
- 2 carrots
- ½ cup almond flour
- ¼ cup pork rinds
- 2 eggs
- 1 teaspoon salt
- ½ teaspoon red pepper
- ⅓ teaspoon ground white pepper
- 1 tablespoon olive oil
- 1 teaspoon dried dill

Directions:
1. Peel the red onion and carrots. Chop the vegetables roughly and transfer them to the food processor.
2. Wash the cauliflower and separate it into the florets.
3. Add the cauliflower florets to a food processor and puree until smooth.
4. Add the eggs and salt. Blend the mixture for 3 minutes, then transfer to a mixing bowl.
5. Add pork rinds, red pepper, ground white pepper, and dill.
6. Blend the mixture until smooth. Form the nuggets from the vegetable mixture and dip them in the almond flour.
7. Spray the Ninja Foodi's insert with olive oil inside.
8. Place the vegetable nuggets in the Ninja Foodi's insert and cook them on the" Sauté" mode for 10 minutes.
9. Once the nuggets are cooked, remove from the Ninja Foodi's insert and serve.

Nutritional Values Per Serving:
Calories: 85; Fat: 5.1g; Carbohydrates: 5.9g; Protein: 5g

Ninja Foodi Popcorn

Prep Time: 5 Minutes
Cook Time: 10 Minutes
Servings: 14

Ingredients:
- 3 tablespoons oil, whatever kind you like
- ½ cup popcorn kernels
- ½ teaspoon salt
- 4 tablespoons butter, salted and room temp

Directions:
1. Measure out a piece of foil that is 4" larger than the diameter of the Ninja Foodi Multi-Cooker Inner Pot and wide enough to be able to fold into a pouch. Tuck the ends under the lip of the inner pot and make multiple holes with a thin sharp object. I used the pointy end of my cake tester. You don't want the holes too big or the butter will just pour out in places.
2. Add the three tablespoons of oil to the inner pot and half cup of popped corn kernel. Turn the Ninja Foodi Multi-Cooker on High Sear/Sauté and cover with Pressure Lid and turn Vent.
3. While you are waiting for the kernel to pop, cut or spread your butter on the foil.
4. When you hear the kernel pop, add in the remaining un popped kernels and the salt. Stir to combine.
5. Close the foil packet and secure by tucking under the lid of the inner pot. Cover with Pressure Lid. Leave the Sear/Sauté on high until to begin to hear the kernels rapidly popping (less than one second between pops), turn the heat down to Medium/Low. Insert a spatula or wooden spoon and stir the bottom to move the kernels around.
6. Once the popping has slowed down to about one pop every few seconds, turn the Ninja Foodi Multi-Cooker off and stir again. If there is any butter left in the foil, shake it over the popcorn and stir.
7. Serve and enjoy!

Nutritional Values Per Serving:
Calories: 78; Fat: 7g; Carbohydrates: 4g; Protein: 1g

Glazed Walnuts

Prep Time: 5 minutes
Cook Time: 4 minutes
Servings: 4

Ingredients:
- ⅓ cup of water
- 6 ounces walnuts
- 5 tablespoon Erythritol
- ½ teaspoon ground ginger
- 3tablespoons psyllium husk powder

Directions:
1. Combine Erythritol and water together in a mixing bowl.
2. Add ground ginger and stir the mixture until the erythritol is dissolved.
3. Transfer the walnuts to the Ninja Foodi's insert and add sweet liquid.
4. Close the Ninja Foodi's lid and cook the dish in the "Pressure" mode for 4 minutes.
5. Remove the walnuts from the Ninja Foodi's insert.
6. Dip the walnuts in the Psyllium husk powder and serve.

Nutritional Values Per Serving:
Calories: 286; Fat: 25.1g; Carbohydrates: 10.4g; Protein: 10.3g

Crispy Onion Rings

Prep Time: 10 minutes
Cook Time: 8 minutes
Servings: 7

Ingredients:
- 1 cup coconut flour
- 1 teaspoon salt
- ½ teaspoon basil
- 1 teaspoon oregano
- ½ teaspoon cayenne pepper
- 3 eggs
- 5 medium white onions
- 3 tablespoons sesame oil

Directions:
1. Combine the coconut flour, salt, basil, oregano, and cayenne pepper together in a mixing bowl.
2. Stir the coconut flour mixture gently. Add the eggs to another bowl and whisk them.
3. Peel the onions and cut them into thick rings.
4. Separate the onion rings and dip them into the egg mixture.
5. Pour the sesame oil in the Ninja Foodi's insert. Preheat it on the "Pressure" mode.
6. Dip the onion rings in the flour mixture. Transfer the onion rings to the Ninja Foodi's insert.
7. Sauté the onions for 2 minutes on each side.
8. Transfer the cooked rings to the paper towel and rest briefly.
9. Season with salt while hot and serve.

Nutritional Values Per Serving:
Calories: 180; Fat: 10.1g; Fiber 7.5g; Carbohydrates: 6.8g; Protein: 5.6g

Chicken Pork Nuggets

Prep Time: 15 minutes
Cook Time: 20 minutes
Servings: 6

Ingredients:
- 2 cups ground chicken
- ½ cup dill, chopped
- 1 egg
- 2 tablespoons pork rinds
- 1 tablespoon heavy cream
- ½ cup almond flour
- 3 tablespoons butter
- 1 tablespoon canola oil
- 1 teaspoon black pepper

Directions:
1. Beat the egg in a suitable mixing bowl.
2. Add the chopped dill and ground chicken. Blend the mixture until it is smooth.
3. Sprinkle the dish with black pepper and cream.

4. Blend the nugget mixture again. Form the nuggets from the meat mixture and dip them in the almond flour and pork rinds.
5. Sprinkle the Ninja Foodi's insert with the canola oil and butter.
6. Set the Ninja Foodi's insert to "Pressure" mode. Once the butter mixture starts to melt, add the nuggets.
7. Close the Ninja Foodi's lid and cook the dish for 20 minutes at Hi.
8. Once done, check if the nuggets are cooked and remove them from the Ninja Foodi's insert.
9. Drain on a paper towel and serve.

Nutritional Values Per Serving:
Calories: 217; Fat: 15.4g; Carbohydrates: 3.1g; Protein: 17.4 g

Japanese Eggs

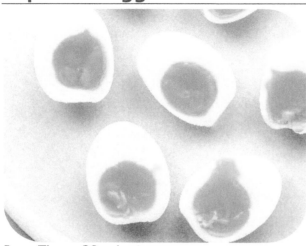

Prep Time: 30 minutes
Cook Time: 20 minutes
Servings: 4

Ingredients:
- 1 cup Chinese master stock
- 4 eggs
- 1 teaspoon salt

Directions:
1. Pour the Chinese master stock in the Ninja Foodi's insert and close the Ninja Foodi's pressure lid.
2. Cook the liquid on the "Pressure" mode for 10 minutes at Lo.
3. Remove the Chinese master stock from the Ninja Foodi's insert and chill it.
4. Meanwhile, place the eggs in the Ninja Foodi's insert.
5. Add water and boil the eggs on the "Pressure" mode for 10 minutes.
6. Once eggs are done, remove from the Ninja Foodi's insert and chill well.
7. Peel the eggs and place them in the Chinese master stock.
8. Leave the eggs in the liquid for 20 minutes.
9. Remove the eggs from the liquid. Cut the eggs into halves.

Nutritional Values Per Serving:
Calories: 134; Fat: 9.7g; Carbohydrates: 2.01g; Protein: 9g

Garlicky Tomato

Prep Time: 10 minutes
Cook Time: 5 minutes
Servings: 5

Ingredients:
- 5 tomatoes
- ¼ cup chives, chopped
- ⅓ cup garlic clove, minced
- ½ teaspoon salt
- ½ teaspoon black pepper
- 1 tablespoon olive oil
- 7 ounces Parmesan cheese

Directions:
1. Wash the tomatoes and slice them into thick slices.
2. Place the sliced tomatoes in the Ninja Foodi's insert.
3. Combine the grated cheese and minced garlic and stir the mixture.
4. Sprinkle the tomato slices with chives, black pepper, and salt.
5. Then sprinkle the sliced tomatoes with the cheese mixture.
6. Close the Ninja Foodi's lid and cook the dish in the "Pressure" mode for 5 minutes at LO.
7. Once done, remove the tomatoes carefully and serve.

Nutritional Values Per Serving:
Calories: 224; Fat: 14g; Carbohydrates: 12.55g; Protein: 13g

Shallots with Mushrooms

Prep Time: 15 minutes
Cook Time: 30 minutes
Servings: 7

Ingredients:
- 9 ounces shallot

- 8 ounces mushrooms
- ½ cup chicken stock
- 1 tablespoon paprika
- ½ tablespoon salt
- ¼ cup cream
- 1 teaspoon coriander
- ½ cup dill, chopped
- ½ cup parsley
- 1 tablespoon Erythritol

Directions:
1. Slice the shallot and chop the mushrooms.
2. Combine the chicken stock, salt, paprika, cream, coriander, and Erythritol in a mixing bowl.
3. Blend the mixture well. Chop the dill and parsley.
4. Pour the cream mixture in the Ninja Foodi's insert.
5. Set the Ninja Foodi's insert to" Sauté" mode and add sliced shallot and chopped mushrooms.
6. Blend the mixture using a wooden spoon. Close the Ninja Foodi's lid and sauté the mixture for 30 minutes.
7. Chop the parsley and dill. Once the dish is done, transfer it to serving plates.
8. Sprinkle the cooked dish with the chopped parsley and dill.
9. Do not stir again before serving it.

Nutritional Values Per Serving:
Calories: 52; Fat: 1g; Carbohydrates: 10.2g; Protein: 3g

Jalapeno Salsa

Prep Time: 5 minutes
Cook Time: 7 minutes
Servings: 10

Ingredients:
1. 8 ounces jalapeno pepper
2. ¼ cup Erythritol
3. 5 tablespoons water
4. 2 tablespoons butter
5. 1 teaspoon paprika

Directions:
1. Wash the jalapeno pepper and remove the seeds.
2. Slice it into thin circles. Sprinkle the sliced jalapeno pepper with paprika and Erythritol.
3. Put the butter and jalaeno mixture into the Ninja Foodi's insert and add water.

4. Set the Ninja Foodi's insert to" Sauté" mode.
5. Once the butter melts, add the sliced jalapeno in the Ninja Foodi's insert.
6. Close the Ninja Foodi's lid and sauté the dish for 7 minutes.
7. Once done, remove the dish from the Ninja Foodi's insert.
8. Cool it and serve.

Nutritional Values Per Serving:
Calories: 28; Fat: 2.5g; Carbohydrates: 7.5g; Protein: 0.4g

Crispy Chicken Skin

Prep Time: 10 minutes
Cook Time: 10 minutes
Servings: 7

Ingredients:
- 1 teaspoon red chili flakes
- 1 teaspoon black pepper
- 1 teaspoon salt
- 9 ounces of chicken skin
- 2 tablespoons butter
- 1 teaspoon olive oil
- 1 teaspoon paprika

Directions:
1. Combine the black pepper, chilli flakes, and paprika together.
2. Stir the mixture and combine it with the chicken skin.
3. Let the mixture rest for 5 minutes. Set the Ninja Foodi's insert to" Sauté" mode.
4. Add the butter to the Ninja Foodi's insert and melt it.
5. Add the chicken skin and sauté it for 10 minutes, stirring frequently.
6. Once the chicken skin gets crunchy, remove it from the Ninja Foodi's insert.
7. Place the chicken skin on the paper towel and drain.
8. Serve warm.

Nutritional Values Per Serving:
Calories: 134; Fat: 11.5g; Carbohydrates: 0.98g; Protein: 7g

Ninja Foodi Spicy Popcorns

Prep Time: 10 minutes
Cook Time: 5 minutes
Servings: 6

Ingredients:
- 1 cup popping corns
- 2 teaspoons ground turmeric
- ½ teaspoon garlic powder
- 6 tablespoons olive oil
- Salt, to taste

Directions:
1. Heat four tablespoons of olive-oil in a Ninja Foodi Multi-cooker and add popping corns in it.
2. Select "Pressure" and close the pressure Lid.
3. Press the "Start/Stop" button and cook for about 5 minutes at HIGH pressure.
4. Take out and set aside.
5. Meanwhile, add remaining olive oil, turmeric, garlic powder and salt in a bowl. Mix well.
6. Pour the mixture on popcorns and toss to coat well.
7. Serve and enjoy!

Nutritional Values Per Serving:
Calories: 143; Fat: 14.1g; Carbohydrates: 5.3g; Protein: 0.3g

Ninja Foodi Spinach Chips

Prep Time: 12 minutes
Cook Time: 10 minutes
Servings: 4

Ingredients:
- ½ teaspoon paprika
- ¼ teaspoon ground cumin
- ¼ teaspoon olive oil
- 2 cups fresh spinach leaves
- Salt, to taste

Directions:
1. Add everything in a large-bowl and mix well. Set aside.
2. Place spinach leaves in Ninja Foodi Multi-cooker and press the "Bake" button.
3. Close the Crisping Lid and press the "Start/Stop" button.
4. Bake for about 10 minutes at 325 degrees F and open the lid.
5. Take out, serve and enjoy!

Nutritional Values Per Serving:
Calories: 7; Fat: 0.4g; Carbohydrates: 0.7g; Protein: 0.5g

Ninja Foodi Cod Sticks

Prep Time: 10 minutes
Cook Time: 15 minutes
Servings: 8

Ingredients:
- 1 cup almond flour
- 2 eggs
- 1 cod fillet, thinly sliced
- 2 teaspoons dried parsley, crushed
- ½ teaspoon cayenne pepper
- Salt and black pepper, to taste

Directions:
1. Add eggs in one bowl and all the other ingredients except cod slices in another bowl. Mix well.
2. Dip cod slices first in egg mixture and then in the other mixture. Set aside.
3. Arrange cod slices in Ninja Foodi Multi-cooker and press the "Bake" button.
4. Close the Crisping Lid and press the "Start/Stop" button.
5. Bake for 6 minutes on each side at 350 degrees F and open the lid.
6. Take out, serve and enjoy!

Nutritional Values Per Serving:
Calories: 111; Fat: 7.9g; Carbohydrates: 3.2g; Protein: 6.9g

Ninja Foodi Cheddar Biscuits

Prep Time: 10 minutes
Cook Time: 15 minutes
Servings: 8

Ingredients:
- ¼ teaspoon baking powder
- ¼ cup butter
- ¼ teaspoon ginger powder
- ¼ teaspoon garlic powder
- 4 eggs
- ¼ cup coconut flour, sifted
- 1 cup cheddar cheese
- Salt, to taste

Directions:
1. Add flour, baking powder, garlic powder and salt in a large bowl. Mix well.
2. Now, add butter and eggs in another bowl. Whisk well.
3. Combine the two mixtures and mix properly. Set aside.
4. Place the batter in Ninja Foodi Multi-cooker and press the "Bake" button.
5. Close the Crisping Lid and press the "Start/Stop" button.
6. Bake for 15-minutes at 400 degrees F and open the lid.
7. Take out, serve and enjoy!

Nutritional Values Per Serving:
Calories: 155; Fat: 13g; Carbohydrates: 3g; Protein: 6.9g

Ninja Foodi Spiced Almonds

Prep Time: 10 minutes
Cook Time: 14 minutes
Servings: 6

Ingredients:
- 2 tablespoons unsweetened applesauce
- 1 cup almonds
- ¼ teaspoon cayenne pepper
- ¼ teaspoon ground cumin
- ½ teaspoon olive oil
- ½ tablespoon water
- ¼ teaspoon ground cinnamon
- ¼ teaspoon red chili powder
- Salt, to taste

Directions:
1. Arrange almonds in Ninja Foodi Multi-cooker and select "Bake".
2. Close the Crisping Lid and press the "Start/Stop" button.
3. Bake for about 10 minutes at 350 degrees F and open the lid.
4. Take out and set aside.
5. Meanwhile, add oil, water and applesauce in a bowl. Mix well.
6. Add in almonds and toss to coat well.
7. Add cinnamon, ground cumin, red chili powder, cayenne pepper and salt in another bowl. Mix well.
8. Arrange almonds again in the Ninja Foodi Multi-cooker and top them with cinnamon mixture.
9. Close the Crisping Lid and press the "Start/Stop" button.
10. Bake them for about 4 minutes at 350 degrees F and open the lid.
11. Take out, serve and enjoy!

Nutritional Values Per Serving:
Calories: 98; Fat: 8.4g; Carbohydrates: 4.2g; Protein: 3.4g

Zucchini Egg Tots

Prep Time: 15 minutes
Cook Time: 9 minutes
Servings: 8

Ingredients:
- 2 medium zucchinis
- 1 egg
- 1 teaspoon salt
- ½ teaspoon baking soda
- 1 teaspoon lemon juice
- 1 teaspoon basil
- 1 tablespoon oregano

- ⅓ cup oatmeal flour
- 1 tablespoon olive oil
- 1 teaspoon minced garlic
- 1 tablespoon butter

Directions:
1. Wash the zucchini and grate it. Beat the egg in a suitable mixing bowl and blend it using a whisk.
2. Add the baking soda, lemon juice, basil, oregano, and flour to the egg mixture.
3. Stir it carefully until smooth. Combine the grated zucchini and egg mixture together.
4. Knead the dough until smooth. Mix olive oil with minced garlic together.
5. Set the Ninja Foodi's insert to "Sauté" mode.
6. Add butter and transfer the mixture to the Ninja Foodi's insert. Melt the mixture.
7. Make the small tots from the zucchini dough and place them in the melted butter mixture.
8. Sauté the dish for 3 minutes on each side.
9. Once the zucchini tots are cooked, remove them from the Ninja Foodi's insert and serve.

Nutritional Values Per Serving:
Calories: 64; Fat: 4.4g; Carbohydrates: 4.35g; Protein: 2g

Shallot Pepper Pancakes

Prep Time: 10 minutes
Cook Time: 15 minutes
Servings: 8

Ingredients:
- 8 ounces shallot, chopped
- 2 tablespoons chives, chopped
- 1 red onion, chopped
- 1 cup coconut flour
- 2 egg
- ¼ cup sour cream
- 1 teaspoon baking soda
- 1 tablespoon lemon juice
- 1 teaspoon salt
- 1 teaspoon cilantro, chopped
- ½ teaspoon basil
- 1 tablespoon olive oil
- 1 bell pepper, chopped

Directions:
1. Chop the shallot and chives and combine them into a mixing bowl.

2. Whisk the eggs in a another bowl and add baking soda and lemon juice.
3. Stir the mixture and add the cream, salt, cilantro, basil, and coconut flour.
4. Blend the mixture well until smooth.
5. Add the vegetables to the egg mixture.
6. Stir it to the batter that forms. Set the Ninja Foodi's insert to" Sauté" mode.
7. Pour the olive oil in the Ninja Foodi's insert and preheat it.
8. Ladle the batter and cook the pancakes for 2 minutes on each side.
9. Keep the pancakes under aluminium foil to keep them warm until all the pancakes are cooked.
10. Serve the pancakes while warm.

Nutritional Values Per Serving:
Calories: 138; Fat: 6g; Carbohydrates: 7.6g; Protein: 4.7g

Ninja Foodi Spicy Peanuts

Prep Time: 5 minutes
Cook Time: 2 hours 40 minutes
Servings: 6

Ingredients:
- ¾ cups peanuts
- 1½ tablespoons chili seasoning mix
- ½ tablespoon butter

Directions:
1. Add peanuts, chili seasoning mix and butter in the pot of Ninja Foodi Multi-cooker. Mix well.
2. Select "Slow Cook" and close the pressure Lid.
3. Press the "Start/Stop" button and cook for about 2 hours and 30 minutes at Lo. Stir after every 30 minutes.
4. Open the lid and cook for 15 minutes.
5. Take out, serve and enjoy!

Nutritional Values Per Serving:
Calories: 134; Fat: 11.1g; Carbohydrates: 6.7g; Protein: 5.6g

Ninja Foodi Banana Cookies

Prep Time: 15 minutes
Cook Time: 20 minutes
Servings: 7

Ingredients:
- 1 banana, mashed
- ¼ cup soymilk
- ½ tablespoon canola oil
- ¼ tablespoon baking powder
- 1 cup white flour

Directions:
1. Add mashed bananas, oil and soymilk in a bowl. Mix well.
2. Add in flour and baking powder. Stir properly.
3. Knead the dough and roll it with the help of a rolling pin.
4. Cut the dough into circles and place them in Ninja Foodi Multi-cooker.
5. Select "Bake" and close the Crisping Lid.
6. Press the "Start/Stop" button and bake for about 20 minutes at 400 degrees F.
7. Open the lid and take out.
8. Serve and enjoy!

Nutritional Values Per Serving:
Calories: 94; Fat: 1.4g; Carbohydrates: 18.3g; Protein: 2.3g

Ninja Foodi Chickpea Crackers

Prep Time: 15 minutes
Cook Time: 20 minutes
Servings: 5

Ingredients:
- ½ cup chickpea flour
- 1 tablespoon yeast
- ¼ cup water
- ¼ teaspoon sesame oil
- ¼ teaspoon baking powder
- 1 teaspoon toasted sesame seeds
- ¼ teaspoon turmeric
- Salt, to taste

Directions:
1. Add baking powder, chickpea flour, sesame seeds, yeast, salt and turmeric in a bowl. Mix well.
2. Add water and oil gradually in the mixture and mix until proper dough is formed.
3. Cover the dough and set aside till the dough rises.
4. Make square shapes out of the dough and place them in Ninja Foodi Multi-cooker.
5. Select "Bake" and close the Crisping Lid.
6. Press the "Start/Stop" button and bake for about 20 minutes at 350 degrees F.
7. Open the Crisping Lid and take out.
8. Serve and enjoy!

Nutritional Values Per Serving:
Calories: 86; Fat: 1.9g; Carbohydrates: 13.4g; Protein: 4.9g

Garlic Pretzels with Ranch Dressing

Prep Time: 6 Minutes
Cook Time: 10 Minutes
Servings: 1

Ingredients:
- 120 grams regular pretzels
- 1 packet Ranch seasoning
- ⅓ teaspoon garlic powder
- 1 tablespoon olive oil
- ⅛ teaspoon cayenne pepper

Directions:
1. Align the Ninja Foodi Multi-Cooker Cook & Crisp Basket with aluminum foil and give it an olive oil spray.
2. In the Ninja Foodi Multi-Cooker Cook & Crisp Basket, place the pretzels and top up with the dry seasonings.
3. Now use an olive oil spray and spray a few coats of it and mix it up until they are fully coated at 390° F.
4. Cook in the Air Crisp Mode for 3 minutes at 390° F, then open the lid and remove the pretzels carefully. Spray a little bit of olive oil and mix up very well.

5. For another 3 minutes cook again then re-move the pretzels carefully or open the lid, spray a bit of olive oil and mix well.
6. Cook it for two more minutes or you can wait until the pretzels are crispy enough!

Nutrition Information per Serving:
Calories: 159; Fat: 4.7g; Carbohydrates: 17.3 g; Protein: 3.4g

Buffalo Cauliflower Platter

Prep Time: 12 Minutes
Cook Time: 12-17 Minutes
Servings: 4

Ingredients:
- 1 medium-sized cauliflower head
- 1 cup of buffalo sauce
- 1 tablespoon of melted butter
- 1 cup of bread crumbs
- Salt to taste

For Sides
- Carrot sticks
- Celery sticks
- 2 tablespoons orange dressing

Directions:
1. Cut the cauliflower into florets and place them in a mixing bowl.
2. Mix the hot sauce and butter in a separate bowl.
3. Now on top of the cauliflower pieces, pour the hot sauce.
4. Let it marinate for 15 minutes, making sure you keep stirring it from time to time. Now in another shallow dish put the bread crumbs and season it with a bit of salt.
5. Now to coat the cauliflower, dip it in the crumb mixture.
6. Place the cauliflower pieces on the Cook & Crisp Basket and make sure to not overlap them.

7. It is recommended to cook this recipe in two batches so that the cauliflower does not get overcrowded.
8. Set the Air Crisp at 390° F and let it cook for about 12 to 15 minutes.
9. Serve these cauliflower buffalo bites with optional orange dressing, carrot, and celery sticks!

Nutritional Values Per Serving:
Calories: 201; Fat: 10.1g; Carbohydrates: 18.5g; Protein: 5.8g

Ninja Foodi Lemon Scones

Prep Time: 10 minutes
Cook Time: 25 minutes
Servings: 3

Ingredients:
- ¾ cup all-purpose flour
- ¼ cup unsweetened soymilk
- 2 tablespoons sugar
- ½ teaspoon lemon extract
- ½ tablespoon sunflower oil
- ½ tablespoon baking powder
- Salt, to taste

Directions:
1. Add wet ingredients in one bowl and dry in-gredients in another. Mix well.
2. Combine the two mixtures and mix until dough is formed.
3. Make spheres out of the mixture and press them with tortilla press.
4. Make triangular shapes out of the dough and place them in Ninja Foodi Multi-cooker.
5. Press the "Bake" button and close the Crisping Lid.
6. Press the "Start/Stop" button and bake for 15 minutes at 400 degrees F.
7. Open the Crisping Lid and take out.
8. Serve and enjoy!

Nutritional Values Per Serving:
Calories: 175; Fat: 3g; Carbohydrates: 33.4g; Protein: 3.8g

Ninja Foodi Herb Crackers

Prep Time: 10 minutes
Cook Time: 20 minutes
Servings: 4

Ingredients:
- ½ cup almond flour
- ½ tablespoon water
- ½ tablespoon herbes de provence
- ¼ tablespoon olive oil
- Salt, to taste

Directions:
1. Add herbes de provence, salt and almond flour in a large bowl. Mix well.
2. Add in olive oil and water. Mix until a soft dough is formed.
3. Make small spheres out of the dough and press them with a tortilla press.
4. Arrange them in the Ninja Foodi Multi-cooker and press the "Bake" button.
5. Close the Crisping Lid and press the "Start/Stop" button.
6. Bake for about 20 minutes at 350 degrees F and open the Crisping Lid.
7. Take out, serve and enjoy!

Nutritional Values Per Serving:
Calories: 154; Fat: 12.6g; Carbohydrates: 3.5g; Protein: 6.8g

Air Crisped Chicken Nuggets

Prep Time: 10 Minutes
Cook Time: 8-10 Minutes
Servings: 6

Ingredients:
- 1 pound minced chicken
- Salt and pepper to taste
- 1 tablespoon olive oil
- 5 tablespoons of season bread crumbs
- 1 tablespoon of panko mix
- 1 tablespoon parmesan cheese (grated)

Directions:
1. At 320° F, preheat the Ninja Foodi Multi-Cooker at Air Crisp Mode for 8 minutes.
2. In a bowl add bread crumbs, panko mix, parmesan cheese, and olive oil.
3. For the seasoning, dump in salt and pepper on the chicken.
4. To ensure the olive oil is evenly coated on all the chicken, put the olive oil well if needed.
5. Shape up the small pieces of chicken that pop out of the batter.
6. Don't add too many chicken chunks at a time into the breadcrumb mixture for the coating purpose. Then place it on the Cook & Crisp Basket and give a slight olive oil spray on the top.
7. Let it Air Crisp for 8 minutes, make sure to turn it halfway until the color is golden!

Nutrition Information per Serving:
Calories: 112; Fat: 3.9g; Carbohydrates: 5.5g; Protein: 10.4g

Coated Onion Rings

Prep Time: 8 Minutes
Cook Time: 9 Minutes
Servings: 2

Ingredients:
- 1 large onion
- 2 tablespoon all-purpose flour
- ½ teaspoon baking powder
- ¼ teaspoon salt
- 1 egg
- ½ cup milk
- 1 teaspoon chili powder

- 4 tablespoons bread crumbs

Directions:
1. Start by slicing the onions into ¼ inch circular rings. The center of the onion needs to be removed.
2. Then divide the slices. Now take a large bowl and place the onion slices on it.
3. Add the flour and toss the slices making sure each piece of onion is coated well.
4. Take another bowl and whisk together the egg, milk, and baking powder.
5. Then add salt, bread crumbs, and chili powder into another bowl.
6. Now dip the coated rings into the egg mixture and then into the bread crumbs until coated well.
7. Spray the Ninja Foodi Multi-Cooker Cook & Crisp Basket with a bit of olive oil or Air Crisp parchment paper can also be used. Place the coated rings into the Ninja Foodi Multi-Cooker Basket until it's full.
8. At 390° F, Air Crisp it for 7 to 8 minutes or wait until the coating is crispy!

Nutritional Values Per Serving:
Calories: 142; Fat: 4.6g; Carbohydrates: 17g; Protein: 7.9g

Ninja Foodi Spicy Cashews

Prep Time: 10 minutes
Cook Time: 2 hours 45 minutes
Servings: 12

Ingredients:
- 2½ cups cashews
- 3 tablespoons chili seasoning mix
- 1½ tablespoons butter

Directions:
1. Add everything in the pot of Ninja Foodi Multi-cooker and mix well.
2. Close the pressure Lid and select "Slow Cook".
3. Press the "Start/Stop" button and cook for about 2 hours and 30 minutes on LOW TEMP.

4. Open the lid and cook for 15 more minutes.
5. Take out, serve and enjoy!

Serving Suggestions: Top with red chili powder before serving.

Variation Tip: You can add cayenne pepper for a stronger taste.

Nutritional Values Per Serving:
Calories: 741; Fat: 61.2g; Carbohydrates: 40.2g; Protein: 18.6g

Chicken Wings

Prep Time: 6 Minutes
Cook Time: 22 Minutes
Servings: 2

Ingredients:
- 8 chicken medium-sized wings
- 2 tablespoons flour
- 1 tablespoon brown sugar
- 1 tablespoon salt
- ½ tablespoon garlic paste
- 1 teaspoon pepper
- ½ tablespoon chili powder
- ½ tablespoon paprika
- 1 tablespoon olive oil

Directions:
1. Use paper towels to pat dry the wings. Add olive oil and spread it on all sides to coat them well.
2. Mix all dry ingredients and put them in the polythene bag. Then add the wings coated with olive oil into the bag and shake well. Now carefully place the wings inside the Ninja Foodi Multi-Cooker Cook & Crisp Basket, making sure they don't overlap each other.
3. Air Crisp them for 8 minutes in Ninja Foodi Multi-Cooker at Air Crisp Mode at 390° F and then flip to the other side and continue cooking for another 8 minutes until you get the desired crispiness.

Nutritional Values Per Serving:
Calories: 200; Fat: 13g; Carbohydrates: 6g; Protein: 10.9g

Sesame Chicken Wings

Prep Time: 10 minutes
Cook Time: 25 minutes
Servings: 4

Ingredients:
- 24 chicken wing segments
- 2 tablespoons toasted sesame oil
- 2 tablespoons Asian-Chile-Garlic sauce
- 2 tablespoons stevia
- 2 garlic cloves, minced
- 1 tablespoon toasted sesame seeds

Directions:
1. Add 1 cup of water to Foodi's inner pot, place reversible rack in the pot in lower portions, place chicken wings in the rack.
2. Place lid into place and seal the pressure valve.
3. Select pressure mode to HIGH and cook for 10 minutes.
4. Make the glaze by taking a large bowl and whisking in sesame oil, Chile-Garlic sauce, choc zero maple syrup and garlic.
5. Once the chicken is done, quick release the pressure and remove the pressure lid.
6. Remove rack from the pot and empty it.
7. Return inner pot to the base.
8. Cover with crisping lid and select Air Crisp mode, adjust the temperature to 375 degrees F, pre-heat for 3 minutes.
9. While the Foodi pre-heats, add wings to the sauce and toss well to coat it.
10. Transfer wings to the basket, leaving any excess sauce in the bowl.
11. Place the basket in Foodi and close with Crisping mode, select Air Crisp mode and let it cook for 8 minutes, gently toss the wings and let it cook for 8 minutes more.
12. Once done, drizzle any sauce and sprinkle sesame seeds.
13. Enjoy.

Nutrition Values Per Serving
Calories: 440; Fat: 32g; Carbohydrates: 12g; Protein: 28g

Chicken Potato Stew

Prep Time: 10-15 Minutes
Cook Time: 8-10 Minutes
Servings: 4-6

Ingredients:
- 2 pounds boneless chicken thighs
- 4 potatoes (coarsely sliced)
- Salt and pepper to taste
- 2-3 peppercorns
- 2 tablespoons olive oil
- 1 tablespoon thyme
- ½ tablespoon onion powder
- 1 teaspoon paprika powder
- 1 tablespoon chopped garlic
- 4 tablespoons chopped onion
- ½ cup chicken broth

Directions:
1. Start by combining thyme paprika, salt and pepper, and onion powder. Now take chicken thighs and season both sides with this spice mix.
2. Put olive oil in a Ninja Foodi Multi-Cooker Pot and select the Air Crisp Mode at 390° F.
3. Air Crisp chicken thigh cuts in Ninja Foodi Multi-Cooker Pot. Cook each side for about 2 to 3 minutes. Now take out the chicken and set it aside.
4. Add onions and chopped garlic to the Ninja Foodi Multi-Cooker Pot. Add the peppercorns and steam for about 2 minutes. Now add chicken broth to it and continue to cook.
5. Now add potatoes and chicken, select Pressure, and cook on High Pressure Ninja Foodi Multi-Cooker setting for 8 minutes. Then allow it to naturally release for about four to 5 minutes then quick release!

Nutritional Values Per Serving:
Calories: 385; Fat: 16.3g; Carbohydrates: 7.7g; Protein: 35.5g

Garlic turkey Breasts

Prep Time: 10 minutes
Cook Time: 17 minutes
Servings: 4

Ingredients:
- ½ teaspoon garlic powder
- 4 tablespoons butter
- ¼ teaspoon dried oregano
- 1-pound turkey breasts, boneless
- 1 teaspoon pepper
- ½ teaspoon salt
- ¼ teaspoon dried basil

Directions:
1. Season turkey on both sides generously with garlic, dried oregano, dried basil, black pepper and salt
2. Select "Sauté" mode on your Ninja Foodi and stir in butter; let the butter melt
3. Add turkey breasts and sauté for 2 minutes on each side
4. Lock the lid and select the "Bake/Roast" setting; bake for 15 minutes at 355 degrees F
5. Serve and enjoy once done.

Nutrition Values Per Serving
Calories: 223; Fat: 13g; Carbohydrates: 5g; Protein: 19g

Lemon Chicken

Prep Time: 5 minutes
Cook Time: 18 minutes
Servings: 4

Ingredients:
- 4 bone-in, skin-on chicken thighs
- Black pepper and salt to taste
- 2 tablespoons butter
- 2 teaspoons garlic, minced
- ½ cup herbed chicken stock
- ½ cup heavy whip cream
- ½ a lemon, juiced

Directions:
1. Season the four chicken thighs generously with black pepper and salt.
2. Set your Ninja Foodi to sauté mode and add oil, let it heat up.
3. Add thigh, Sauté on both sides for 6 minutes.
4. Remove thigh to a platter and keep it on the side.
5. Add garlic, cook for 2 minutes.
6. Whisk in chicken stock, heavy cream, lemon juice and gently stir.
7. Bring the mix to a simmer and reintroduce chicken.
8. Lock and secure the Ninja Foodi's lid and cook for 10 minutes on "HIGH" pressure.
9. Release pressure over 10 minutes.
10. Serve and enjoy.

Nutrition Values Per Serving
Calories: 294; Fat: 26g; Carbohydrates: 4g; Protein: 12g

Chicken and Broccoli

Prep Time: 10 minutes
Cook Time: 20 minutes
Servings: 4

Ingredients:
- 3 pounds boneless chicken, cut into thin strips
- 1 tablespoon olive oil
- 1 yellow onion, peeled and chopped
- ½ cup beef stock
- 1-pound broccoli florets
- 2 teaspoons toasted sesame oil
- 2 tablespoons arrowroot

For Marinade
- 1 cup coconut aminos
- 1 tablespoon sesame oil
- 2 tablespoons fish sauce
- 5 garlic cloves, peeled and minced
- 3 red peppers, dried and crushed
- ½ teaspoon Chinese five-spice powder
- Toasted sesame seeds, for serving

Directions:

1. Take a suitable and mix in coconut aminos, fish sauce, 1 tablespoon sesame oil, garlic, five-spice powder, crushed red pepper and stir
2. Stir in chicken strips to the bowl and toss to coat
3. Keep it on the side for 10 minutes
4. Select "Sauté" mode on your Ninja Foodi and stir in oil, let it heat up, add onion and stir cook for 4 minutes
5. Stir in chicken and marinade, stir cook for 2 minutes
6. Add stock and stir
7. Lock the pressure lid of Ninja Foodi and cook on "HIGH" pressure for 5 minutes
8. Release pressure naturally over 10 minutes
9. Mix arrowroot with ¼ cup liquid from the pot and gently pour the mixture back to the pot and stir
10. Place a steamer basket in the Ninja Foodi's pot and stir in broccoli to the steamer rack, Lock and secure the Ninja Foodi's lid.
11. Then cook on "HIGH" pressure mode for 3 minutes more, quick-release pressure
12. Divide the dish between plates and serve with broccoli, toasted sesame seeds and enjoy.

Nutritional Values Per Serving:
Calories: 433; Fat: 27g; Carbohydrates: 8g; Protein: 20g

Ham-Stuffed Turkey Rolls

Prep Time: 10 minutes
Cook Time: 20 minutes
Servings: 8

Ingredients:
- 4 tablespoons fresh sage leaves
- 8 ham slices
- 8 6 ounces each turkey cutlets
- Black pepper and salt to taste
- 2 tablespoons butter, melted

Directions:
1. Season turkey cutlets with black pepper and salt
2. Roll turkey cutlets and wrap each of them with ham slices tightly
3. Coat each roll with butter and gently place sage leaves evenly over each cutlet

4. Transfer them to your Ninja Foodi
5. Lock and secure the Ninja Foodi's lid and select the "Bake/Roast" mode, bake for 10 minutes a 360 degrees F
6. Open the Ninja Foodi's lid and gently give it a flip, Lock and secure the Ninja Foodi's lid again and bake for 10 minutes more
7. Once done, serve and enjoy.

Nutrition Values Per Serving
Calories: 467; Fat: 24g; Carbohydrates: 1.7g; Protein: 56g

Ninja Foodi Turkey & Beans Wrap

Prep Time: 10 minutes
Cook Time: 13 minutes
Servings: 3

Ingredients:
- ¼ pound lean ground turkey
- ¼ teaspoon ground cumin
- 3 butternut lettuce leaves
- ¼ teaspoon garlic powder
- 1½ tablespoons tomato sauce
- ¼ cup cooked black beans
- ¼ cup chopped onion
- 1½ tablespoons extra-virgin olive oil
- Salt and black pepper, to taste

Directions:
1. Add turkey, onion, tomato sauce, garlic powder, cumin, salt and pepper in a large bowl. Mix well.
2. Meanwhile, heat oil in a Ninja Foodi Multi-cooker and add turkey mixture in it.
3. Select "Pressure" and press the "Start/Stop" button at LO.
4. Cook for 10 minutes and stir in tomato sauce and beans.
5. Cook for about 3 minutes and take out.
6. Divide the mixture evenly on lettuce leaves and serve.

Nutritional Values Per Serving:
Calories: 356; Fat: 28.7g; Carbohydrates: 14.8g; Protein: 12.5g

Shredded Chicken Salsa

Prep Time: 5 minutes
Cook Time: 20 minutes
Servings: 4

Ingredients:
- 1-pound chicken breast, boneless
- ¾ teaspoon cumin
- ½ teaspoon salt
- Pinch of oregano
- Pepper to taste
- 1 cup chunky salsa

Directions:
1. Season chicken with spices and add to Ninja Foodi.
2. Cover with salsa and lock lid, cook on "HIGH" pressure for 20 minutes.
3. Quick-release pressure.
4. Add chicken to a platter and shred the chicken.
5. Serve and enjoy.

Nutrition Values Per Serving
Calories: 125; Fat: 3g; Carbohydrates: 2g; Protein: 22g

Chicken Tortilla

Prep Time: 15 minutes
Cook Time: 15 minutes
Servings: 4

Ingredients:

- 1 tablespoon avocado oil
- 1-pound pastured boneless chicken breasts
- ½ cup orange juice
- 2 teaspoons gluten-free Worcestershire sauce
- 1 teaspoon garlic powder
- 1 teaspoon salt
- ½ teaspoon chilli powder
- ½ teaspoon paprika

Directions:
1. Select "Sauté" mode on your Ninja Foodi and stir in oil; let the oil heat up
2. Add chicken on top, take a suitable and stir in remaining ingredients mix well
3. Pour the mixture over chicken
4. Lock and secure the Ninja Foodi's lid, then cook on "HIGH" pressure for 15 minutes
5. Release pressure naturally over 10 minutes
6. Shred the chicken and serve over salad green shells such as cabbage or lettuce
7. Enjoy.

Nutrition Values Per Serving
Calories: 338; Fat: 23g; Carbohydrates: 10g; Protein: 23g

Paprika Chicken

Prep Time: 10 minutes
Cook Time: 5 minutes
Servings: 4

Ingredients:
- 4 chicken breasts, skin on
- Black pepper and salt, to taste
- 1 tablespoon olive oil
- ½ cup sweet onion, chopped
- ½ cup heavy whip cream
- 2 teaspoons smoked paprika
- ½ cup sour cream
- 2 tablespoons fresh parsley, chopped

Directions:
1. Season the four chicken breasts with black pepper and salt
2. Select "Sauté" mode on your Ninja Foodi and add oil; let the oil heat up
3. Add chicken and sear both sides until properly browned, should take about 15 minutes
4. Remove chicken and transfer them to a plate
5. Take a suitable skillet and place it over medium heat; stir in onion.
6. Sauté for 4 minutes until tender
7. Stir in cream, paprika and bring the liquid to a simmer.

8. Return chicken to the skillet and alongside any juices
9. Transfer the whole mixture to your Ninja Foodi and lock lid, cook on "HIGH" pressure for 5 minutes
10. Release pressure naturally over 10 minutes
11. Stir in sour cream, serve and enjoy.

Nutrition Values Per Serving
Calories: 389; Fat: 30g; Carbohydrates: 4g; Protein: 25g

Ninja Foodi Lime Chicken Soup

Prep Time: 10 minutes
Cook Time: 8 hours
Servings: 5

Ingredients:
- ¼ cup fresh lime juice
- 4 garlic cloves, minced
- ½ teaspoon oregano
- 1 onion, chopped
- 4 cups chicken broth
- 2 cups boneless chicken, cubed
- 1 tomato, chopped
- ½ teaspoon red chili powder
- ¾ cup chopped mushrooms
- ½ teaspoon ground cumin
- Salt and black pepper, to taste

Directions:
1. Add everything in the pot of Ninja Foodi Multi-cooker and select "Slow Cook".
2. Close the pressure Lid and press the "Start/Stop" button.
3. Cook for about 8 hours at LOW TEMP and open the lid.
4. Take out the chicken cubes and shred them properly.
5. Stir the shredded chicken in the Slow Cook and take out.
6. Serve and enjoy!

Nutritional Values Per Serving:
Calories: 157; Fat: 5.4g; Carbohydrates: 4.9g; Protein: 21g

Jalapeno Chicken Nachos

Prep Time: 8-9 Minutes
Cook Time: 8-9 Minutes
Servings: 2

Ingredients:
- 1 cup tortillas chips
- 1 pound minced chicken
- ¼ cup BBQ sauce
- Salt to taste
- ½ cup chicken broth
- ½ cup cheddar cheese
- ½ corn
- 2 tablespoons chopped olives
- ½ cup sliced jalapeno
- 1 coarsely cut onion
- Coriander to garnish

Directions:
1. Add the chicken, broth, and salt to a Ninja Foodi Multi-Cooker. For 8 minutes, Pressure Cook it on High and releases the pressure when finished quickly.
2. Stir in BBQ sauce after draining the liquid.
3. At 390° F, preheat the Ninja Foodi Multi-Cooker at Air Crisp Mode. Take Ninja Foodi Multi-Cooker Cook & Crisp Basket and align the parchment paper.
4. Place tortilla chips on the base. Now give a layer of shredder BBQ chicken and corn and top it off with cheddar cheese evenly.
5. For about 5 to 10 minutes place it in the Ninja Foodi Multi-Cooker and wait until cheese is melted. Then add olives, onions, jalapenos slice to the desired amount. Follow it by adding fresh coriander!

Nutritional Values Per Serving:
Calories: 550; Fat: 25.5g; Carbohydrates: 29.7g; Protein: 55g

Ninja Foodi Chicken & Carrot Stew

Prep Time: 10 minutes
Cook Time: 6 hours
Servings: 3

Ingredients:
- 2 (¼ pound) boneless chicken breasts, cubed
- ½ cup chopped onions
- ½ teaspoon dried thyme
- 1 garlic clove, minced
- 1½ cup cubed carrots
- ½ cup chopped tomatoes
- 1 cup chicken broth
- Salt and black pepper, to taste

Directions:
1. Add everything in the Ninja Foodi Multi-cooker and select "Slow Cook".
2. Close the pressure Lid and press the "Start/Stop" button.
3. Cook for about 6 hours at HIGH TEMP and take out.
4. Serve and enjoy!

Nutritional Values Per Serving:
Calories: 226; Fat: 6.4g; Carbohydrates: 16.6g; Protein: 25g

Ninja Foodi Turkey Stew

Prep Time: 20 minutes
Cook Time: 48 minutes
Servings: 6

Ingredients:
- 1½ pounds cooked turkey, chopped
- 1 cup pumpkin puree
- 2 tablespoons olive oil
- 2 cups chopped tomatoes
- 4 scallions, chopped
- 1½ cups water
- 2 teaspoons grated ginger
- Salt and black pepper, to taste

Directions:
1. Heat 1 tablespoon olive oil in a Ninja Foodi Multi-cooker and select "Sear/Sauté".
2. Press the "Start/Stop" button and sauté scallions and ginger in it for about 3 minutes. Take out and set aside.
3. Now, add remaining oil in the pot of Ninja Foodi Multi-cooker and cook turkey in it for about 3 minutes.
4. Stir in scallion mixture and cook for about 2 minutes.
5. Add in remaining ingredients and simmer for about 40 minutes.
6. Dish out and serve hot.

Nutritional Values Per Serving:
Calories: 777; Fat: 25.8g; Carbohydrates: 6.8g; Protein: 123g

Ninja Foodi Duck Stew

Prep Time: 10 minutes
Cook Time: 24 minutes
Servings: 3

Ingredients:
- 1 teaspoon canola oil
- ½ cup chopped carrot
- ¾ teaspoon minced garlic
- 1 cup beans, rinsed and drained
- ½ pound duck breasts, sliced
- ½ cup chopped celery
- ½ cup chopped onion
- ½ cup chicken broth
- 1 cup diced tomatoes
- Salt and pepper, to taste

Directions:
1. Heat oil inNinja Foodi Multi-cooker and select "Pressure".
2. Press the "Start/Stop" button and cook duck breasts in it for about 7 minutes.

3. Take out the duck and sauté celery, carrot, onion and garlic in the skillet for about 7 minutes.
4. Return duck in the pot of Ninja Foodi and stir in broth, beans and tomatoes.
5. Close the pressure Lid and cook for about 10 minutes.
6. Open the pressure Lid and take out.
7. Serve and enjoy!

Nutritional Values Per Serving:
Calories: 159; Fat: 5g; Carbohydrates: 9.4g; Protein: 19.2g

Ninja Foodi Chicken & Salsa Chili

Prep Time: 10 minutes
Cook Time: 8 hours 5 minutes
Servings: 4

Ingredients:
- 1 cup salsa
- ¾ cup water
- ½ jalapeno pepper, minced
- ½ teaspoon ground cumin
- 1 teaspoon chili powder
- ½ pound boneless chicken breast
- 1 garlic clove, minced
- ½ onion, chopped
- ½ avocado, chopped
- 1½ green bell peppers, chopped
- Salt and black pepper, to taste

Directions:
1. Add chicken, garlic, cumin, salsa, and water in a Ninja Foodi Multi-cooker and select "Slow Cook".
2. Close the pressure Lid and press the "Start/Stop" button.
3. Cook for about 6 hours on HIGH TEMP and open the lid.
4. Meanwhile, heat the non-stick skillet and cook onions, jalapeno pepper and bell pepper in it for about 5 minutes.
5. Now, take the chicken out of the Ninja Foodi Multi-cooker and shred it properly.

6. Place it back in the Slow Cook along with onion mixture, chili powder, avocado, salt and pepper. Mix well.
7. Cook for about 2 hours and take out.
8. Serve and enjoy!

Nutritional Values Per Serving:
Calories: 239; Fat: 9.8g; Carbohydrates: 20.7g; Protein: 19.9g

Ninja Foodi Cranberry Chicken

Prep Time: 20 minutes
Cook Time: 25 minutes
Servings: 6

Ingredients:
- 1½ pounds boneless chicken thighs
- 1 cup fresh cranberries
- ¼ cup chopped onion
- 2 tablespoons unsweetened applesauce
- 2 tablespoons fresh ginger, minced
- 2 tablespoons olive oil
- 1 cup chicken broth
- Salt and black pepper, to taste

Directions:
1. Heat oil in Ninja Foodi Multi-cooker and select "Pressure".
2. Press the "Start/Stop" button and add chicken, salt and pepper to it.
3. Cook for 5 minutes per side and take out the chicken. Set aside.
4. Sauté onions for about 3 minutes in the same pot and stir in broth.
5. Add cranberries after 5 minutes, followed by applesauce and cook for about 7 minutes.
6. Pour the cranberry mixture on the chicken and serve immediately.

Nutritional Values Per Serving:
Calories: 308; Fat: 22.1g; Carbohydrates: 4.1g; Protein: 21.1g

Ninja Foodi Ground Turkey

Prep Time: 10 minutes
Cook Time: 8 minutes
Servings: 6

Ingredients:
- 1 tablespoon sesame oil
- 2 pounds lean ground turkey
- 1 onion, chopped
- ½ cup soy sauce
- ½ cup chicken broth
- 2 teaspoons ground ginger
- 3 garlic cloves, minced
- Salt and black pepper, to taste

Directions:
1. Add oil in a Ninja Foodi Multi-cooker and press the "Sear" button.
2. Press the "Start/Stop" button and sauté onion in it for about 3 minutes.
3. Add in garlic and turkey and mash the mixture with a fork.
4. Stir in chicken broth, soy sauce, salt and pepper and cook for about 5 minutes.
5. Take out and serve hot.

Nutritional Values Per Serving:
Calories: 262; Fat: 13.3g; Carbohydrates: 4.3g; Protein: 31.8g

Glazed Chicken & Vegetables

Prep Time: 8-10 Minutes
Cook Time: 20-25 Minutes
Servings: 2

Ingredients:
- ½ pound chicken thighs boneless
- 2 tablespoons soya sauce
- 2 teaspoons Worcestershire sauce
- 2 tablespoons brown sugar
- 4 crushed garlic cloves
- 1 pound bag of frozen mixed vegetables
- 1 tablespoon vinegar optional
- 1 tablespoon olive oil
- Black pepper to taste

Directions:
1. Start by adding soya sauce, Worcestershire sauce, brown sugar and ginger garlic in a closable container or zip lock bag. Now add chicken in it and seal to coat it well with the marinade. Let it rest in the fridge for two to three hours.
2. Oil spray the Ninja Foodi Multi-Cooker Cook & Crisp Basket. Now put vegetables and chicken in the Ninja Foodi Multi-Cooker Cook & Crisp Basket.
3. Give a spray of olive oil again and sprinkle just a pinch of salt if preferred.
4. Air Crisp it for about 25 minutes at 390° F.
5. When the chicken reaches 165 °F internally, serve it!

Nutritional Values Per Serving:
Calories: 397; Fat: 11.3g; Carbohydrates: 25.5g; Protein: 27.4g

Turkey Cutlets

Prep Time: 10 minutes
Cook Time: 15 minutes
Servings: 4

Ingredients:
- 1 teaspoon Greek seasoning
- 1-pound turkey cutlets
- 2 tablespoons olive oil
- 1 teaspoon turmeric powder
- ½ cup almond flour

Directions:
1. Take a suitable and stir in turmeric powder, Greek seasoning, almond flour and mix well.
2. Dredge turkey cutlets in the bowl and let it sit for 30 minutes.

3. Select "Sauté" mode on your Ninja Foodi and stir in oil, heat up.
4. Add cutlets and Sauté for 2 minutes.
5. Lock and secure the Ninja Foodi's lid and cook on Low-Medium Pressure for 20 minutes.
6. Release pressure naturally over 10 minutes.
7. Take the dish out, serve and enjoy.

Nutrition Values Per Serving
Calories: 340; Fat: 19g; Carbohydrates: 3.7g; Protein: 36g

Ninja Foodi Spinach Chicken

Prep Time: 10 minutes
Cook Time: 10 minutes
Servings: 4

Ingredients:
- 1 pound chicken tenders
- 2 tablespoons sour cream
- 2 garlic cloves, minced
- 1¼ cups chopped spinach
- 2 tablespoons olive oil
- ¼ cup parmesan cheese, shredded
- Salt and black pepper, to taste

Directions:
1. Heat half of the oliveoil in a Ninja Foodi Multi-cooker and add chicken, salt and pepper in it.
2. Select "Pressure" and press the "Start/Stop" button.
3. Cook for about 2-minutes per side at Hi and take out the chicken. Set aside.
4. Add remaining oil in the pot of Ninja Foodi and sauté garlic in it for about 1 minute.
5. Add spinach, cream, and cheese in the skillet and cook for about 2 minutes.
6. Place chicken in the Ninja Foodi Multi-cooker's pot and simmer for about 5 minutes.
7. Take out and serve hot.

Serving Suggestions: Serve with onion rings on the top.

Variation Tip: Mozzarella cheese can also be used.

Nutritional Values Per Serving:
Calories: 301; Fat: 17.1g; Carbohydrates: 1.6g; Protein: 34.3g

Ninja Foodi Chicken Broth

Prep Time: 10 minutes
Cook Time: 3 hours
Servings: 3

Ingredients:
- 1½ pounds chicken
- 1 bay leaf
- 1 celery stalk, chopped
- ¼ teaspoon dried rosemary, crushed
- 1 carrot, chopped
- ¼ teaspoon dried thyme
- 4 peppercorns
- 1 onion, quartered
- 4 cups cold water

Directions:
1. Add everything in a Ninja Foodi Multi-cooker and select "Slow Cook".
2. Close the pressure Lid and press the "Start/Stop" button at Hi.
3. Simmer for about 3 hours and open the lid.
4. Take out and set aside.
5. Strain the broth and serve hot.

Nutritional Values Per Serving:
Calories: 1281; Fat: 25.3g; Carbohydrates: 5.9g; Protein: 241.6g

Ninja Foodi Basil Pesto Chicken

Prep Time: 20 minutes
Cook Time: 30 minutes
Servings: 4

Ingredients:
- 4 boneless chicken breasts
- 3 garlic cloves, minced
- ½ cup pine nuts
- 2 cups fresh basil leaves
- ½ teaspoon red pepper flakes
- ½ cup olive oil
- Salt and black pepper, to taste

Directions:
1. Add olive oil, garlic, pine nuts, basil and red pepper flakes in a food processor. Pulse well.
2. Now, arrange chicken breasts in the pot of Ninja Foodi Multi-cooker and pour basil mixture on it.
3. Select "Bake" and close the Crisping Lid.
4. Press the "Start/Stop" button and bake for about 30 minutes at 375 degrees F.
5. Open the Crisping Lid and take out.
6. Serve and enjoy!

Nutritional Values Per Serving:
Calories: 603; Fat: 47.3g; Carbohydrates: 3.4g; Protein: 43.4g

Ninja Foodi Duck Fajita Platter

Prep Time: 10 minutes
Cook Time: 25 minutes
Servings: 4

Ingredients:
- 1 pound duck breasts, sliced
- ½ green bell pepper, chopped
- ½ red bell pepper, chopped
- 1 onion, sliced
- 2 tablespoons olive oil
- 1 teaspoon garlic powder
- 1 teaspoon ground cumin
- 2 teaspoons chili powder
- ½ teaspoon dried oregano
- Salt, to taste

Directions:
1. Add duck breasts, green bell pepper, red bell pepper and garlic powder in a large bowl. Mix well.
2. Add in chili powder, cumin, onion, olive oil, oregano and salt in the bowl. Toss to coat well.
3. Place the duck breasts in the pot of Ninja Foodi Multi-cooker and select "Bake".
4. Close the Crisping Lid and press the "Start/Stop" button.
5. Bake for about 25 minutes at 400 degrees F and open the lid.
6. Take out and serve hot.

Nutritional Values Per Serving:
Calories: 237; Fat: 12g; Carbohydrates: 6.7g; Protein: 26.1g

Ninja Foodi Barbeque Chicken Drumsticks

Prep Time: 10 minutes
Cook Time: 8 hours
Servings: 4

Ingredients:
- 12 chicken drumsticks
- 2 tablespoons red chili powder
- 1 teaspoon onion powder
- 1 teaspoon garlic powder
- 4 tablespoons honey
- 2 tablespoons apple cider vinegar
- 1 cup barbeque sauce

- 1 tablespoon paprika
- ½ tablespoon ground cumin
- Salt and black pepper, to taste

Directions:
1. Add everything except honey in a Ninja Foodi Multi-cooker and select "Slow Cook".
2. Close the pressure Lid and press the "Start/Stop" button.
3. Cook for about 8 hours at HIGH TEMP and open the lid.
4. Take out the drumsticks and pour honey on them.
5. Serve and enjoy!

Nutritional Values Per Serving:
Calories: 416; Fat: 9.1g; Carbohydrates: 44.4g; Protein: 39g

Ninja Foodi Duck Broth

Prep Time: 10 minutes
Cook Time: 8 hours
Servings: 16

Ingredients:
- 1 roasted duck, meat removed
- 2 teaspoons apple cider vinegar
- 8 cups water
- 2 carrots, chopped
- 2 onions, chopped
- Salt, to taste

Directions:
1. Add duck bones in a Ninja Foodi Multi-cooker and sprinkle some salt on it.
2. Add in remaining ingredients and select "Slow Cook".
3. Cover the pressure Lid and press the "Start/Stop" button.
4. Cook for 8 hours at low TEMP and open the lid.
5. Take out the broth and serve.

Nutritional Values Per Serving:
Calories: 21; Fat: 0.7g; Carbohydrates: 2g; Protein: 1.8g

Parmesan Chicken

Prep Time: 8-10 Minutes
Cook Time: 7 Minutes
Servings: 4

Ingredients:
- 1 medium-sized chicken breast
- ½ cup chicken broth
- 1 teaspoon garlic powder
- 1 teaspoon salt
- ⅛ teaspoon pepper

Italian seasoning:
- 1 teaspoon chili flakes
- ½ cup cream
- 1 tablespoon cornstarch
- ½ cup grated parmesan cheese
- Water as required to mix the cornstarch
- 1 tablespoon basil leaves paste

Directions:
1. Take a board and lay your chicken breast on it, pat dry it, and cut into halves. Take a half breast and cut it cross-sectionally to make two out of every half. Hammer the bread to flatten it with a pounder. A full breast yields four hammered fillets. Season it with salt, pepper, and garlic powder generously.
2. Leave it to marinate for 30 minutes in the bottom of the Ninja Foodi Multi-Cooker Bowl. Turn on the Air Crisp Mode at 390° F and cook the fillet from both sides.
3. Now while the chicken is cooking, prepare seasoning. Start to melt the butter, add salt and pepper, lemon juice, crushed garlic, and some parmesan cheese and add other seasonings according to your taste.
4. Once cooked, take out the fillets. Pour the chicken broth along with the prepared sauce in the same Ninja Foodi Multi-Cooker Bowl and cover it with a Ninja Foodi Multi-Cooker Pressure Lid and then into the seal position, place the toggle switch.
5. Pressure Cook it for 5 minutes on High Pressure and do a pressure quick release. Remove it again.
6. Now at 390° F in Air Crisp Mode for 10 minutes. Let the chicken baste with your garlic parmesan sauce to infuse the flavors!

Nutritional Values Per Serving:
Calories: 338; Fat: 22.6g; Carbohydrates: 25.9g; Protein: 7.1g

Chicken Vegetable Soup

Prep Time: 8 Minutes
Cook Time: 3 Minutes
Servings: 2

Ingredients:
- ½ pound boneless chicken thigh (bite-size cuts)
- 1 diced carrot
- 1 chopped onion
- 1 teaspoon garlic
- ½ cup boiled pasta
- 4 cups broth
- 1 teaspoon salt
- ¾ teaspoon white pepper
- 1 tablespoon soy sauce
- 1 teaspoon oregano
- ¼ teaspoon red chili powder
- 2 bay leaves
- ¼ cup corn flour slurry

Directions:
1. In the Ninja Foodi Multi-Cooker Pot, add carrots, onion, garlic, bay leaves then add the bite-size chicken cuts.
2. Now season it with salt, white pepper, oregano, red chili powder, and soy sauce and pour in the chicken broth.
3. Give it a good stir. Now set the valve to Seal and install the Ninja Foodi Multi-Cooker Pressure Lid.
4. Select the Pressure function and set it to High. Press the start button and set the timer for 2 minutes. Usually, the pressure takes about 10 minutes to start building up.
5. Once it beeps, allow the pressure to naturally release for about 10 minutes after the completion of pressure cooking. And quickly release any remaining pressure by setting the valve to venting.
6. Now take out the bay leaves and discard them, select the option Steam and, let the soup simmer for another 3 to 5 minutes.
7. Pour in slurry and stir it well. Give it a boil until it's completely thickened. Serve instantly!

Nutritional Values Per Serving:
Calories: 389; Fat: 10.3g; Carbohydrates: 16g; Protein: 31.9g

Pulled Barbecue Chicken

Prep Time: 6 Minutes
Cook Time: 9-10 Minutes
Servings: 2

Ingredients:
- 1 pound chicken breast
- 1 cup broth
- 4 tablespoons BBQ sauce
- ½ teaspoon liquid smoke
- Salt and pepper to taste

Directions:
1. Now inside the Ninja Foodi Multi-Cooker Pot, place the chicken breast and sprinkle a little salt and pepper on both sides.
2. Then, add in broth over the chicken breasts, and install the Pressure Lid and switch the vent knob to Seal properly. Select the High option of the Ninja Foodi Multi-Cooker Pressure setting function for about 8 minutes and then press the stop button.
3. Quickly release the pressure on food after the timer goes off and then remove the lid carefully.
4. Make sure that broth is reduced to half. Then add the barbecue sauce and let it cook on Air Crisp Mode at 390° F for 5 to 10 minutes. Make sure to shred it a bit with a spatula or fork.
5. Add the liquid smoke and it's good to go!

Nutritional Values Per Serving:
Calories: 311; Fat: 4g; Carbohydrates: 6.1g; Protein: 34.7g

Honey Garlic Chicken

Prep Time: 12 Minutes
Cook Time: 15-20 Minutes
Servings: 2

Ingredients:
- 1 pound bone-in chicken pieces
- 1 tablespoon sesame oil
- ¼ cup broth
- 2 tablespoons honey
- 2 tablespoons soya sauce
- ½ tablespoon apple cider vinegar
- 1 teaspoon chopped garlic
- Salt to taste
- Pepper to taste
- 1 tablespoon cornstarch
- ¼ cup water

Directions:
1. Combine honey, broth, soy sauce, and apple cider vinegar in a bowl and whisk it well.
2. Meanwhile, add chicken and garlic to the Ninja Foodi Multi-Cooker Pot. Steam for 2 to 3 minutes and pour the chicken broth mixture.
3. Now Seal the pressure lid and secure the valve and set Ninja Foodi Multi-Cooker Pressure Cook at High and cook for 8 minutes.
4. Whisk cornstarch water together in a small bowl and prepare a slurry while the chicken is being cooked.
5. After 8 minutes, allow natural release of pressure for about ten min and then turn it to quick release manually. Carefully open the lid and take it out then set Ninja Foodi Multi-Cooker Pressure Cook Low setting and mix the slurry into the sauce and keep stirring. Allow it to thicken for about 2 to 3 minutes. Coat all the chicken well.
6. Garnish it with some fresh green onion and a few sesame seeds!

Nutritional Values Per Serving:
Calories: 219; Fat: 13.4g; Carbohydrates: 11.7g; Protein: 22.8g

Mexican Chicken with Rice

Prep Time: 12-15 Minutes
Cook Time: 10 Minutes
Servings: 4

Ingredients:
- 1 pound chicken breasts boneless
- 1 cup uncooked rice
- Salt to taste
- ½ teaspoon chili flakes
- 2-3 minced garlic cloves
- 1 can black beans
- ¼ cup corn
- ½ cup chicken broth
- ¼ cup cheese
- 2 diced onion
- 1 tablespoon olive oil

Directions:
1. Turn on the Ninja Foodi Multi-Cooker Mode at 390° F and then add olive oil.
2. Add onions, garlic powder, chicken cubes, chili flakes, and salt once oil is hot and cook it until the protein changes its color.
3. Dump in black beans and corn alongside chicken broth after turning off the Ninja Foodi Multi-Cooker Pot. Stir well together.
4. Now on top of that, sprinkle uncooked rice and by using the back of the spoon, submerge it into the liquid but don't stir it.
5. Put the lid back on and close the steam valve for nine minutes. After that let it naturally release pressure.
6. Lift the lid, fluff up the rice mixture and add cheese on top, mix it gently and set the top back again for about 3 minutes for the cheese to melt!

Nutritional Values Per Serving:
Calories: 31.5; Fat: 14.4g; Carbohydrates: 31.5g; Protein: 61g

Maple Glazed Pork Chops

Prep Time: 45 minutes
Cook Time: 12 minutes
Servings: 4

Ingredients:
- 2 tablespoons choc zero maple syrup
- 4 tablespoons mustard
- 2 tablespoons garlic, minced
- Black pepper and salt to taste
- 4 pork chops
- Cooking spray

Directions:
1. Mix the choc zero maple syrup, mustard, garlic, black pepper and salt in a suitable.
2. Marinate the choc zero maple syruped pork chops in the mixture for 20 minutes.
3. Place the pork chops on the Ninja Foodi basket.
4. Put the basket inside the pot. Seal with the crisping lid.
5. Set it to air crisp. Cook at 350 degrees F for about 12 minutes, flipping halfway through.

Nutritional Values Per Serving:
Calories: 348; Fat: 23.3g; Carbohydrate: 14g; Protein: 21.1g

Rosemary Lamb Chops

Prep Time: 20 minutes
Cook Time: 10 minutes
Servings: 6

Ingredients:
- 3 lb. lamb chops
- 4 rosemary sprigs
- Salt to taste
- 1 tablespoon olive oil
- 2 tablespoons butter
- 1 tablespoon tomato paste
- 1 cup beef stock
- 1 green onion, sliced

Directions:
1. Season the lamb chops with rosemary, black pepper and salt.
2. Pour in the olive oil and stir in the butter to the Ninja Foodi. Set it to sauté.
3. Add the lamb chops and cook for one minute per side. Stir in the rest of the ingredients.
4. Stir well. Cover the pot. Set it to pressure. Cook at "HIGH" pressure for 5 minutes.
5. Release the pressure naturally.
6. Serve with pickled onions.

Nutritional Values Per Serving:
Calories: 484; Fat: 23g; Carbohydrate: 1.2g; Protein: 64.4g

Beef Sirloin Steak

Prep Time: 5 minutes
Cook Time: 17 minutes
Servings: 4

Ingredients:
- 3 tablespoons butter
- ½ teaspoon garlic powder
- 1-2 pounds beef sirloin steaks
- Black pepper and salt to taste
- 1 garlic clove, minced

Directions:
1. Select "Sauté" mode on your Ninja Foodi and add butter; let the butter melt
2. Stir in beef sirloin steaks
3. Sauté for 2 minutes on each side
4. Add garlic powder, garlic clove, salt, and pepper
5. Lock and secure the Ninja Foodi's lid and cook on "High" pressure for 15 minutes
6. Release pressure naturally over 10 minutes
7. Transfer prepare Steaks to a serving platter, enjoy.

Nutritional Values Per Serving:
Calories: 246; Fat: 13g; Carbohydrates: 2g; Protein: 31g

Ninja Foodi Pork Shoulder Roast

Prep Time: 10 minutes
Cook Time: 10 hours
Servings: 14

Ingredients:
- 4 pounds pork shoulder roast
- 4 carrots, peeled and sliced
- 4 onions, sliced
- 4 tablespoons Italian seasonings
- Salt and black pepper, to taste

Directions:
1. Add pork shoulder, Italian seasonings, salt and pepper in a large bowl. Mix-well and set aside for about 4 hours.
2. Now, place carrots and onions in the bottom of Ninja Foodi Multi-cooker and add marinated pork shoulder in it.
3. Select "Slow Cook" and close the pressure Lid.
4. Press the "Start/Stop" button and cook for about 10 hours on low TEMP.
5. Open the pressure Lid and take out.
6. Serve and enjoy!

Nutritional Values Per Serving:
Calories: 365; Fat: 27.6g; Carbohydrates: 5.1g; Protein: 22.3g

Ninja Foodi Carrot & Pork Stew

Prep Time: 10 minutes
Cook Time: 8 hours
Servings: 4

Ingredients:
- 1 pound pork meat, trimmed
- 1½ onions, sliced thinly
- 3 carrots, sliced thinly
- ¾ cup vegetable broth
- Salt and black pepper, to taste

Directions:
1. Add everything in a Ninja Foodi Multi-cooker and mix well.
2. Select "Slow Cook" and press the "Start/Stop" button.
3. Close the pressure Lid and cook for about 8 hours.
4. Open the lid and take out.
5. Serve and enjoy!

Nutritional Values Per Serving:
Calories: 465; Fat: 34.8g; Carbohydrates: 21.2g; Protein: 17.1g

Ninja Foodi Beef Casserole

Prep Time: 10 minutes
Cook Time: 8 hours
Servings: 3

Ingredients:
- ½ pound beef steak, chopped
- ½ cup chopped tomatoes
- ½ onion, chopped
- ¼ cup beef broth
- Salt and black pepper, to taste

Directions:
1. Add everything in a Ninja Foodi Multi-cooker and select "Slow Cook".
2. Cover the lid and press the "Start/Stop" button.
3. Cook for about 8-hours on LOW TEMP and open the lid.
4. Take out, serve and enjoy!

Nutritional Values Per Serving:
Calories: 156; Fat: 4.9g; Carbohydrates: 3g; Protein: 23.8g

Corned Beef

Prep Time: 10 minutes
Cook Time: 60 minutes
Servings: 4

Ingredients:
- 4 pounds beef brisket
- 2 garlic cloves, peeled and minced
- 2 yellow onions, peeled and sliced
- 11 ounces celery, sliced
- 1 tablespoon dried dill
- 3 bay leaves
- 4 cinnamon sticks, cut into halves
- Black pepper and salt to taste
- 17 ounces of water

Directions:
1. Take a suitable and stir in beef, add water and cover, let it soak for 2-3 hours
2. Drain and transfer to the Ninja Foodi
3. Stir in celery, onions, garlic, bay leaves, dill, cinnamon, dill, salt, pepper and the rest of the water to the Ninja Foodi
4. Stir and combine it well
5. Lock and secure the Ninja Foodi's lid, then cook on "HIGH" pressure for 50 minutes
6. Release pressure naturally over 10 minutes
7. Transfer meat to cutting board and slice, divide amongst plates and pour the cooking liquid alongside veggies over the servings
8. Enjoy.

Nutritional Values Per Serving:
Calories: 289; Fat: 21g; Carbohydrates: 14g; Protein: 9g

Korean Ribs

Prep Time: 10 minutes
Cook Time: 45 minutes
Servings: 6

Ingredients:
- 1 teaspoon olive oil
- 2 green onions, cut into 1-inch length
- 3 garlic cloves, smashed
- 3 quarter-sized ginger slices
- 4 pounds beef short ribs, 3 inches thick, cut into 3 rib portions
- ½ cup of water
- ½ cup coconut aminos
- ¼ cup dry white wine
- 2 teaspoons sesame oil
- Mince green onions for serving

Directions:
1. Set your Ninja Foodi to "Sauté" mode and stir in oil, let it shimmer
2. Add green onions, garlic, ginger, Sauté for 1 minute
3. Stir in short ribs, water, amines, wine, sesame oil, and stir until the ribs are coated well
4. Lock and secure the Ninja Foodi's lid, then cook on "HIGH" pressure for 45 minutes
5. Release pressure naturally over 10 minutes
6. Remove short ribs from pot and serve with the cooking liquid
7. Enjoy.

Nutritional Values Per Serving:
Calories: 423; Fat: 35g; Carbohydrates: 4g; Protein: 22g

Beef Bourguignon

Prep Time: 10 minutes
Cook Time: 30 minutes
Servings: 4

Ingredients:
- 1-pound stewing steak
- ½-pound bacon
- 5 medium carrots, diced
- 1 large red onion, peeled and sliced
- 2 garlic cloves, minced
- 2 teaspoons salt
- 2 tablespoons fresh thyme
- 2 tablespoons fresh parsley, chopped
- 2 teaspoons ground pepper
- ½ cup beef broth
- 1 tablespoon olive oil
- 1 tablespoon sugar-free maple syrup

Directions:
1. Select "Sauté" mode on your Ninja Foodi and stir in 1 tablespoon of oil, allow the oil to heat up.
2. Pat your beef dry and season it well.

3. Stir in beef into the Ninja Foodi in batches and Sauté them until nicely browned up.
4. Slice up the cooked bacon into strips and add the strips to the pot.
5. Add onions as well and brown them.
6. Stir in the rest of the listed ingredients and lock up the lid.
7. Cook for 30 minutes on "HIGH" pressure.
8. Allow the pressure to release naturally over 10 minutes. Enjoy.

Nutritional Values Per Serving:
Calories: 416; Fats: 18g; Carbohydrates: 12g; Protein:27g

Cheesy Beef Casserole

Prep Time: 7 Minutes
Cook Time: 15-20 Minutes
Servings: 6

Ingredients
- 1 pound ground beef
- 2 cups frozen vegetable
- 1 teaspoon pea salt
- 1 cup rice
- 4 minced garlic cloves
- Black pepper to taste
- 1 cup beef stalk
- ¼ cup cheddar cheese
- ¼ cup whipping cream
- 2 tablespoons melted butter
- ½ cup bread crumbs

Directions:
1. Turn the Ninja Foodi Multi-Cooker on High Pressure setting and add the ground beef, salt, pepper, onion. Cook a bit and then add rice.
2. When cooking, shred the beef and stir occasionally. Add in chopped garlic after the beef is partially cooked and cook it for two to three more minutes.
3. Pour in beef stalk. Put on a pressure lid and Seal the valve. Cook for 2 minutes on Ninja Foodi Multi-Cooker High Pressure, then let it naturally release pressure for 5 minutes when time is up, and release the remaining pressure manually.
4. Add vegetables and cream. Stir it and mix well.
5. Put back the Ninja Foodi Multi-Cooker Pressure Lid and check the valve to Vent. While you get the topping mixed up, let it sit for 3 to 5 minutes, and keep a check on the vegetables to make sure they are cooked properly.

6. Once cooked, put a layer of cheese on it.
7. Combine melted butter, bread crumbs and mix it well. Top up the casserole with this layer.
8. On top of the casserole cut the topping in an even layer, select the Ninja Foodi Multi-Cooker function at 390° F for 8 to 10 minutes and put down the Cook & Crisp lid. And keep checking from time to time until the cheese is melted. Serve and enjoy!

Nutritional Values Per Serving:
Calories: 505; Fat: 26.8g; Carbohydrates: 24.8g; Protein: 32.5g

Veggies & Beef Stew

Prep Time: 10 minutes
Cook Time: 10 minutes
Servings: 4

Ingredients:
- 1-pound beef roast
- 4 cups beef broth
- 3 garlic cloves, chopped
- 1 carrot, chopped
- 2 celery stalks, chopped
- 2 tomatoes, chopped
- ½ white onion, chopped
- ¼ teaspoon salt
- ⅛ teaspoon black pepper

Directions:
1. Stir in listed ingredients to your Ninja Foodi and lock lid, cook on "HIGH" pressure for 10 minutes
2. Quick-release pressure.
3. Open the Ninja Foodi's lid and shred the bee using forks
4. Serve and enjoy.

Nutritional Values Per Serving:
Calories: 211; Fat: 7g; Carbohydrates: 2g; Protein: 10g

Carne Guisada

Prep Time: 10 minutes
Cook Time: 45 minutes
Servings: 4

Ingredients:
- 3 pounds beef stew
- 3 tablespoon seasoned salt
- 1 tablespoon oregano chilli powder
- 1 tablespoon cumin
- 1 pinch crushed red pepper
- 2 tablespoons olive oil
- ½ medium lime, juiced
- 1 cup beef bone broth
- 3 ounces tomato paste
- 1 large onion, sliced

Directions:
1. Trim the beef stew to taste into small bite-sized portions
2. Toss the beef stew pieces with dry seasoning
3. Select "Sauté" mode on your Ninja Foodi and stir in oil; allow the oil to heat up
4. Add seasoned beef pieces and brown them
5. Combine the browned beef pieces with the rest of the ingredients
6. Lock the Ninja foodi's lid and cook on "HIGH" pressure for 3 minutes
7. Release the pressure naturally
8. Enjoy.

Nutritional Values Per Serving:
Calories: 274; Fats: 12g; Carbohydrates: 11g; Protein: 33g

Beef Lasagna

Prep Time: 10 minutes
Cook Time: 10-15 minutes
Servings: 4

Ingredients:
- 2 small onions
- 2 garlic cloves, minced

- 1-pound ground beef
- 1 large egg
- 1 and ½ cups ricotta cheese
- ½ cup parmesan cheese
- 1 jar 25 ounces0 marinara sauce
- 8 ounces mozzarella cheese, sliced

Directions:
1. Select "Sauté" mode on your Ninja Foodi and stir in beef, brown the beef
2. Add onion and garlic
3. Add parmesan, ricotta, egg in a small dish and keep it on the side
4. Stir in sauce to browned meat, reserve half for later
5. Sprinkle mozzarella and half of ricotta cheese into the browned meat
6. Top with remaining meat sauce
7. For the final layer, add more mozzarella cheese and the remaining ricotta
8. Stir well
9. Cover with a foil transfer to Ninja Foodi
10. Lock and secure the Ninja Foodi's lid, then cook on "HIGH" pressure for 8-10 minutes
11. Quick-release pressure
12. Drizzle parmesan cheese on top
13. Enjoy.

Nutritional Values Per Serving:
Calories: 365; Fats: 25g; Carbohydrates: 6g; Protein: 25g

Braised Lamb Shanks

Prep Time: 20 minutes
Cook Time: 46 minutes
Servings: 4

Ingredients:
- 2 tablespoons olive oil
- 4 lamb shanks
- Black pepper and salt to taste
- 4 cloves garlic, minced
- ¾ cup dry red wine
- 1 teaspoon dried basil
- ¾ teaspoons dried oregano
- 28 oz. crushed tomatoes

Directions:
1. Turn the Ninja Foodi to sauté. Stir in the oil. Season the lamb with Black pepper and salt.
2. Cook until brown. Remove and set aside. Add the garlic and cook for 15 seconds.
3. Pour in the wine. Simmer for 2 minutes. Stir in the basil, oregano and tomatoes.
4. Put the lamb back to the pot. Seal the pot. Set it to pressure.
5. Cook at "HIGH" pressure for 45 minutes. Release the pressure naturally.
6. Serve over polenta.

Nutritional Values Per Serving:
Calories: 790; Fat: 31g; Carbohydrate: 18.3g; Protein: 96.8g

Beef Prime Roast

Prep Time: 10 minutes
Cook Time: 45 minutes
Servings: 4

Ingredients:
- 2 pounds chuck roast
- 1 tablespoon olive oil
- 1 teaspoon salt
- 1 teaspoon black pepper
- 1 teaspoon onion powder
- 1 teaspoon garlic powder
- 4 cups beef stock

Directions:
1. Place roast in Ninja Food pot and season it well with black pepper and salt
2. Stir in oil and set the pot to Sauté mode, sear each side of the roast for 3 minutes until slightly browned
3. Add beef broth, onion powder, garlic powder, and stir
4. Lock and secure the Ninja Foodi's lid, then cook on "HIGH" pressure for 40 minutes.
5. Once done, naturally release the pressure over 10 minutes
6. Open the Ninja Foodi's lid and serve hot. Enjoy.

Nutritional Values Per Serving:
Calories: 308; Fat: 22g; Carbohydrates: 2g; Protein: 24g

Sweet and Sour Pork

Prep Time: 15-20 Minutes
Cook Time: 15 Minutes
Servings: 4

Ingredients:
- 2 pound boneless pork
- 3 teaspoons paprika powder
- 1 can pineapple chunks
- 1 chopped onion
- 1 teaspoon chopped green chili
- 2 tablespoons apple cider vinegar
- 2 tablespoons brown sugar
- 2 tablespoons Worcestershire sauce
- Salt to taste
- 2 tablespoons of cornstarch
- ½ cup sliced green onion

Directions:
1. Add pork to a large shallow dish, and sprinkle paprika all over it. Turn on the Sauté setting and adjust for Medium heat. Pour in oil and sear the pork cuts.
2. Now invert the pork to the Ninja Foodi Multi-Cooker and set it on high Pressure Cook setting. Now add onion, green pepper, soya sauce, vinegar, salt, brown sugar, and pineapple juice to the Ninja Foodi Multi-Cooker. Lock the lid and block the pressure Release valve.
3. Cook in your Ninja Foodi Multi-Cooker Pressure Cook on High For 10 minutes. Then release the pressure quickly and click on Slow Cook setting and adjust on High and let it simmer. Now take a small bowl and make a slurry with cornstarch and water.
4. Stir it slowly into the pork gravy, then add pineapple and cook until the sauce thickens up for about one to 2 minutes and sprinkle refreshing green onion on it!

Nutritional Values Per Serving:
Calories: 403; Fat: 12.7g; Carbohydrates: 31.8g; Protein: 42.8g

Ninja Foodi Lamb & Kale Stew

Prep Time: 10 minutes
Cook Time: 6 hours 5 minutes
Servings: 10

Ingredients:
- 3 pounds lamb meat, cubed
- 1 teaspoon dried thyme
- 1 celery stalk, chopped
- 2 tablespoons olive oil
- 1 teaspoon dried basil
- 1 cup chopped tomatoes
- 2 onions, chopped
- ½ cup chopped carrots
- 2 cups water
- 2 garlic cloves, minced
- 10 cups fresh kale, chopped
- Salt and black pepper, to taste

Directions:
1. Heat oil in the pot of Ninja Foodi Multi-cooker and add lamb, salt and pepper in it.
2. Select "Slow Cook" and press the "Start/Stop" button.
3. Cook for about 5 minutes and take out. Set aside.
4. Now, add lamb with all the other ingredients in a Ninja Foodi Slow Cook and close the pressure Lid.
5. Cook for about 6 hours at HIGH TEMP and open the lid.
6. Take out, serve and enjoy!

Nutritional Values Per Serving:
Calories: 350; Fat: 20.9g; Carbohydrates: 10.6g; Protein: 27.8g

Ninja Foodi Beef Chili

Prep Time: 10 minutes
Cook Time: 6 hours
Servings: 3

Ingredients:

- ¾ pound lean ground beef
- ¼ tablespoon garlic, minced
- ½ tablespoon dried basil
- ¼ onion, chopped
- 1 tablespoon tomato paste
- ½ tablespoon chili powder
- ¼ cup chicken broth
- ½ tablespoon balsamic vinegar
- 2 tablespoons water
- ¾ tablespoon capers
- ½ tablespoon dried thyme
- ¼ tablespoon cayenne pepper
- Salt, to taste

Directions:
1. Add everything in a Ninja Foodi Multi-cooker and select "Slow Cook".
2. Press the "Start/Stop" button and close the pressure Lid.
3. Cook for about 6 hours on low TEMP and open the lid.
4. Take out and serve hot.

Nutritional Values Per Serving:
Calories: 231; Fat: 7.6g; Carbohydrates: 3.5g; Protein: 35.5g

Ninja Foodi Lamb & Carrot Stew

Prep Time: 10 minutes
Cook Time: 9 hours
Servings: 3

Ingredients:
- ¾ pound lamb chops, trimmed
- ½ cup vegetable broth
- 2½ carrots, chopped
- 1 onion, chopped
- Salt and black pepper, to taste

Directions:
1. Add all the ingredients in Ninja Foodi Multi-cooker and mix well. Select "Slow Cook".
2. Cover the pressure Lid and press the "Start/Stop" button.
3. Cook for about 9 hours on LOW TEMP and open the lid.
4. Serve and enjoy!

Nutritional Values Per Serving:
Calories: 320; Fat: 8.6g; Carbohydrates: 24.6g; Protein: 34.8g

Ninja Foodi Lamb Chops with Tomatoes

Prep Time: 10 minutes
Cook Time: 8 hours
Servings: 4

Ingredients:
- 1 pound lamb chops
- 3 tablespoons mixed herbs
- 1 cup water
- 1½ cups chopped tomatoes
- Salt and black pepper, to taste

Directions:
1. Mix everything in Ninja Foodi Multi-cooker and cover the lid.
2. Select "Slow Cook" and press the "Start/Stop" button.
3. Cook for about 8 hours at low TEMP and open the lid.
4. Take out, serve and enjoy!

Nutritional Values Per Serving:
Calories: 258; Fat: 8.9g; Carbohydrates: 10.2g; Protein: 34.2g

Ninja Foodi Plum & Beef Salad

Prep Time: 20 minutes
Cook Time: 10 minutes
Servings: 6

Ingredients:

- 2 pounds beef, trimmed
- 2 teaspoons unsweetened applesauce
- 8 plums, thinly sliced
- 4 tablespoons olive oil
- Salt and black pepper, to taste

Directions:
1. Add 1 tablespoon salt, olive oil and pepper in a large bowl. Mix well.
2. Add in beef and toss to coat well.
3. Place beef in Ninja Foodi Multi-cooker and select "Pressure".
4. Close the pressure Lid and press the "Start/Stop" button.
5. Cook for about 5 minutes at LO per side and open the lid.
6. Take out the beef in a bowl and add in remaining ingredients. Mix properly.
7. Serve and enjoy!

Nutritional Values Per Serving:
Calories: 402; Fat: 19g; Carbohydrates: 10.9g; Protein: 46.5g

Ninja Foodi Filling Beef Dish

Prep Time: 10 minutes
Cook Time: 10 minutes
Servings: 4

Ingredients:
- 2 tablespoons olive oil
- 4 garlic cloves, minced
- 1 pound beef sirloin steak, chopped
- 3 tablespoons low-sodium soy sauce
- 2 cups fresh kale, chopped
- 2 cups carrots, chopped
- Salt and pepper, to taste

Directions:
1. Heat olive oil in Ninja Foodi Multi-cooker and select "Pressure".
2. Sauté garlic in it for about 1 minute and press the "Start/Stop" button.
3. Add in black pepper and beef. Stir well and cook for about 4 minutes at LO.
4. Stir in kale, soy sauce, salt and carrots and cook for about 5 minutes.
5. Take out and serve hot.

Nutritional Values Per Serving:
Calories: 318; Fat: 14.1g; Carbohydrates: 10.7g; Protein: 36.8g

Ninja Foodi Minced Beef with Tomatoes

Prep Time: 10 minutes
Cook Time: 10 hours
Servings: 4

Ingredients:
- ¾ cup chopped tomatoes
- ½ cup water
- ½ pound minced beef
- 1½ tablespoons mixed herbs
- Salt and black pepper, to taste

Directions:
1. Mix all the ingredients in a Ninja Foodi Multi-cooker and select "Slow Cook".
2. Close the pressure Lid and press the "Start/Stop" button.
3. Cook for about 8-hours on LOW TEMP and open the lid.
4. Take out, serve and enjoy!

Nutritional Values Per Serving:
Calories: 116; Fat: 3.7g; Carbohydrates: 2.3g; Protein: 17.7g

Ninja Foodi Ground Beef Soup

Prep Time: 20 minutes
Cook Time: 21 minutes
Servings: 6

Ingredients:
- 1 pound lean ground beef
- 1 ginger, minced
- ½ pound fresh mushrooms, sliced
- 1 onion, chopped

- 2 tablespoons soy sauce
- 1 garlic clove, minced
- 4 cups chicken broth
- Salt and black pepper, to taste

Directions:
1. Add beef in a large Ninja Foodi Multi-cooker, press the "Broil" button and cook for about 2 minutes.
2. Press the "Start/Stop" button and stir in mushrooms, garlic and onion and cook for about 4 minutes.
3. Add in remaining ingredients and cook for 15 minutes on low heat.
4. Take out, serve and enjoy!

Nutritional Values Per Serving:
Calories: 186; Fat: 5.8g; Carbohydrates: 4.4g; Protein: 27.9g

Ninja Foodi Steak Fajitas

Prep Time: 10 minutes
Cook Time: 8 hours
Servings: 3

Ingredients:
- 1 pound beef, trimmed and sliced
- 1¼ cups salsa
- 1 tablespoon fajita seasoning
- ½ bell pepper, sliced
- ½ onion, sliced
- Salt and black pepper, to taste

Directions:
1. Place salsa in the bottom of Ninja Foodi Multi-cooker and top it with fajita seasoning, onion, beef, bell pepper, salt and pepper.
2. Stir well and select "Slow Cook".
3. Close the pressure Lid and cook for about 8 hours.
4. Open the lid and take out.
5. Serve and enjoy!

Nutritional Values Per Serving:
Calories: 369; Fat: 9.9g; Carbohydrates: 20.3g; Protein: 49.9g

Ninja Foodi Spinach Beef Soup

Prep Time: 10 minutes
Cook Time: 30 minutes
Servings: 4

Ingredients:
- 1 tablespoon olive oil
- 4 cups spinach, chopped
- 1 onion, chopped
- 4 cups chicken broth
- 1 pound ground beef
- 1 teaspoon ground ginger
- 1 cup chopped carrots
- Salt and black pepper, to taste

Directions:
1. Add oil and beef in Ninja Foodi Multi-cooker and select "Pressure".
2. Press the "Start/Stop" button and cook for about 5-minutes.
3. Add in broth, spinach, carrots, onions, ginger, salt and pepper. Mix well.
4. Cook for about 25 minutes at LO and take out.
5. Serve and enjoy!

Nutritional Values Per Serving:
Calories: 310; Fat: 12.1g; Carbohydrates: 7.6g; Protein: 40.7g

Tomahawk Rib-Eye Steak

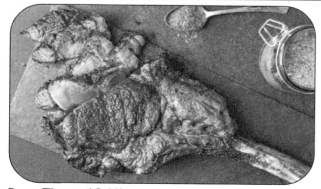

Prep Time: 10 Minutes
Cook Time: 52 Minutes
Servings: 1-2

Ingredients:
- 1 tomahawk rib-eye steak, about 1 ¾ inches thick
- Kosher salt, to taste
- Freshly ground pepper, to taste
- 1 small head garlic
- 2 tablespoons oil, plus more for drizzling (canola or grapeseed)
- 4 tablespoons (½ stick) unsalted butter
- 4 large sprigs fresh thyme

Directions:
1. Pat dry the tomahawk steak with paper towels.
2. Season steak very liberally with kosher salt and freshly ground pepper. Let the steak come to room temperature.
3. Meanwhile, prepare the garlic. Trim off the top ¼inch of the garlic bulb. Drizzle with the oil and add a pinch of salt, then wrap in a foil tent, and cook in Ninja Foodi Multi-Cooker on Pressure Cook low Setting the garlic for 30 minutes, until the cloves are soft. Remove from the Ninja Foodi Multi-Cooker and allow to cool.
4. Moisten a paper towel and wrap it around the steak's rib bone, then wrap aluminum foil around the paper towel.
5. In Ninja Foodi Multi-Cooker, lay the tomahawk steak into the Ninja Foodie Multi-Cooker and Sear for 3 minutes in 2 tablespoon oil without touching it, on selecting Sear Setting at Medium.
6. Using tongs and the bone as a handle, turn the steak over and cook for another 3 minutes without touching it on Sear setting on Medium Setting. Using tongs and the bone as a handle, sear the short side of the steak opposite the bone, about 3 minute.
7. Sear tomahawk rib-eye steak on both sides.
8. Transfer the steak to a rimmed baking sheet and place again in the Ninja Foodi Multi-Cooker, and set it at Roast Setting at 400°F and roast for 10 minutes, or until the desired doneness is reached.
9. Use an instant-read thermometer to measure the steak's internal temperature—125° F for rare, 135° F for Medium-rare, or 145° F for Medium.
10. Make paste of butter and garlic.
11. When the steak is ready, take it out of the Ninja Foodi Multi-Cooker, and use a spoon to paste the butter and garlic over the steak. Turn the steak, and paste again, about 1 minute total. Transfer the steak to a cutting board, tent it with foil, and let it rest 10 minutes.
12. Then add this cutted steaks into Ninja Foodie Multi-Cooker and Cook tomahawk rib-eye steak again in Ninja Foodi Multi-Cooker on High Pressure Mode for 5 minutes.
13. Then take out steaks and top with butter and garlic. You can, simply spoon the butter and garlic over the steak. Serve and enjoy.

Nutritional Values Per Serving:
Calories: 1990; Fat: 145g; Carbohydrates: 7g; Protein: 160g

Beef Onion Pattie Burgers

Prep Time: 6 Minutes
Cook Time: 12-15 Minutes
Servings: 4

Ingredients:
- 1 pound ground beef
- 8 tablespoons onion soup mix

For Assembling:
- Cheese slices
- Onion rings
- Lettuce leaves
- Ketchup
- 4 burger buns

Directions:
1. Combine the ground beef and onion soup mix in a large bowl to make four patties.
2. Oil spray the parchment paper-lined Ninja Foodi Multi-Cooker Cook & Crisp Basket evenly.
3. Place the patties in Ninja Foodi Multi-Cooker and turn on the Air Crisp function at 390° F for 5 minutes. Once done, assemble the burgers as per your likings.
4. Again, place the burgers in the Ninja Foodi Multi-Cooker. Turn the burgers carefully and for an additional 6 to 7 minutes Air Crisp it, until the internal temperature reaches 165° F.

Nutritional Values Per Serving:
Calories: 329; Fat: 13.7g; Carbohydrates: 23.9g; Protein: 27.3g

Roasted Beef

Prep Time: 9-10 Minutes
Cook Time: 25-30 Minutes
Servings: 2

Ingredients:

- 1 pound beef round steaks
- Salt to taste
- Pepper to taste
- 2 tablespoons onion powder
- 1 tablespoon garlic powder
- ½ teaspoon red pepper
- ½ teaspoon paprika
- 1 teaspoon cumin powder
- 1 tablespoon coriander powder
- 1 tablespoon butter

Directions:
1. Combine the dry ingredients with butter and apply them generously to the meat.
2. Select the option Broil and let the beef be broiled for 25 minutes on the Ninja Foodi Multi-Cooker reversable rack in a Low position. Turn off the Ninja Foodi Multi-Cooker and keep the lid closed for about 20 to 25 minutes.
3. Remove it and let it rest for 10 minutes, slice it finely and serve!

Nutritional Values Per Serving:
Calories: 327; Fat: 15.4g; Carbohydrates: 16.5g; Protein: 27.7g

Char Siu Pork

Prep Time: 25 Minutes
Cook Time: 1.5 hours
Servings: 2

Ingredients:
- 1 pound pork fillet
- ½ cup chicken broth
- 2 tablespoons soy sauce
- ¼ cup ketchup
- 2 tablespoons honey
- 3 tablespoons bean paste
- 1 teaspoon garlic paste
- 1 teaspoon ginger paste
- 1 teaspoon five-spice powder
- ¼ cup fresh coriander leaves

Directions:
1. Start by combining honey, bean paste, soya sauce, ketchup, ginger garlic, and the five-spice powder into a large shallow dish. Now add pork to the dish and turn to coat evenly in the dry mix.
2. Transfer pork in a Ninja Foodi Multi-Cooker Pot. Take Ninja Foodi Multi-Cooker Pressure Cook and add chicken broth to it. Seal the pressure lid and close the valve for 75

minutes, adjust your Ninja Foodi Multi-Cooker Pressure Cook setting on High, and then after time allow for 10 minutes to pressure to release naturally. Then quickly release the remaining pressure manually.

3. When pork is done, cut the pork coarsely.

4. Then turn on Sauté setting and let it cook for 2 to 3 minutes at Low heat. Press cancel and top up with fresh coriander!

Nutritional Values Per Serving:
Calories: 521; Fat: 15g; Carbohydrates: 34.6g; Protein: 59.7g

Beef Stew

Prep Time: 9-10 hours
Cook Time: 25-30 Minutes
Servings: 2-3

Ingredients
- 1 pound beef cuts
- 2 carrots (coarsely sliced)
- 2 potatoes (coarsely sliced)
- 4 tablespoons gram flour
- Salt 1 teaspoon
- 1 teaspoon dried thyme
- 1 teaspoon pepper
- 1 diced onions
- 1 cup red wine
- 2 tablespoons Worcestershire sauce
- 4-5 minced garlic cloves
- 1 cup sliced mushrooms
- 1 tablespoon olive oil

Directions:
1. Into a container add flour, thyme, pepper, and salt. Take the beef cuts and add them into the flour mixture to coat them well.

2. In the inner pot of Ninja Foodi Multi-Cooker, add olive oil and turn the Pressure Cook on High. Add floured beef when the oil is very hot. Sear it from all sides for about 10 minutes.

3. Then add chopped garlic and onion into the Ninja Foodi Multi-Cooker Pot.

4. Now with the help of wine, deglaze the Ninja Foodi Multi-Cooker Pot and remove the brown bits from the bottom with a non-stick spatula.

5. Once the wine thickens, add beef broth and Worcestershire sauce to the inner pot of Ninja Foodi Multi-Cooker. Put on the pressure lid and turn the valve to Seal and cook in Ninja Foodi Multi-Cooker High Pressure Setting for 20 minutes. Release the pressure when time is up.

6. Cut carrots, mushrooms, potatoes, and onions into slices while beef is being Pressure Cooked. After the pressure has been released, add in vegetables, put on the Pressure Lid and Seal the valve.

7. Pressure Cook it for 2 minutes and serve. Enjoy!

Nutritional Values Per Serving:
Calories: 390; Fat: 7.8g; Carbohydrates: 25.2g; Protein: 38.4g

Lamb Shanks

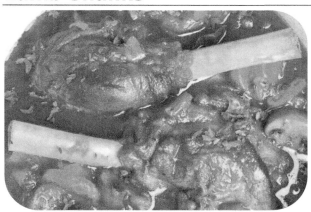

Prep Time: 35-40 Minutes
Cook Time: 1 hour and 20 Minutes
Servings: 1

Ingredients:
- 2 skinless lamb shanks
- 1 teaspoon ginger garlic paste
- 1 teaspoon oregano
- ¾ teaspoon paprika
- ¾ teaspoon salt
- ½ teaspoon black pepper
- ½ teaspoon ground cumin powder
- 1 tablespoon brown sugar
- 1 onion
- 2 small carrots
- 2 bay leaves
- ½ cup red wine
- 2 cups beef stock
- 2 tablespoons cornstarch
- ¼ cup water
- ¼ cup olive oil
- 1 tablespoon olive oil (for cooking)

Directions:
1. Combine lamb, salt, pepper, oregano, ginger garlic paste, paprika, cumin powder, brown sugar, and in a large bowl, and then add oil to it. Coat it well and let it marinate for 30 minutes, or over a night.
2. Click on Pressure Cook on Low setting and heat the Ninja Foodi Multi-Cooker Pot. Now pour in olive oil and place shanks side by side. Cook for 15 minutes and then remove lamb shanks once they are brown and put them aside.
3. Now add bay leaves, carrots, onions, and the remaining leftover marinade to the Ninja Foodi Multi-Cooker Pot and cook it until onions become translucent. Cook for about 5 minutes.
4. To deglaze the pot, add red wine and make sure to scrape out all the bits that are stuck on the bottom. Now return the shanks to the pot for 10 minutes, simmer it to reduce by half.
5. Pour in the stock, and cook for 30 minutes at High Pressure on Ninja Foodi Multi-Cooker and lock pressure lid.
6. And then naturally release the pressure once it's cooked. Now remove shanks and put them aside.
7. Make a slurry of cornstarch with water in a bowl and add it to the pot.
8. Switchback the Ninja Foodi Multi-Cooker Instant Pot to Low Pressure setting until sauce reaches the desired thickness. Now return lamb to the Ninja Foodi Multi-Cooker Pot and let it sit in the sauce until it's ready to be served!

Nutritional Values Per Serving:
Calories: 995; Fat: 69.3g; Carbohydrates: 56g; Protein: 12.2g

Maple Lamb Chops

Prep Time: 6-8 Minutes
Cook Time: 12-15 Minutes
Servings: 2

Ingredients:
- 4 lamb chops
- 2 tablespoons maple syrup
- 1 tablespoon rosemary
- 2 tablespoons extra-virgin olive oil
- 1 teaspoon garlic paste
- Salt and pepper to taste
- 8-10 fresh mint leaves

Directions:
1. Add oil, maple syrup, rosemary, and garlic to a bowl to mix the ingredients well. Now add pepper and salt to it. Dump in lamb chops and coat it well, leave it to marinate in the refrigerator for 2 to 4 hours.
2. Preheat Ninja Foodi Multi-Cooker at 375° F at Bake option for 10 minutes.
3. Place the marinated lamb and close the lids. Let the chops cook for 6 minutes on the Bake. Then flip the chops by opening the top lid and then cook them for six more minutes with a closed lid.
4. Once cooked, its internal temperature should reach 145° F. Now plate it out and add chopped mint and maple syrup on top of it!

Nutritional Values Per Serving:
Calories: 508; Fat: 24.9g; Carbohydrates: 19.6g; Protein: 29.4g

Pork Tenderloin

Prep Time: 5 Minutes
Cook Time: 15-20 Minutes
Servings: 1

Ingredients:
- 1 pound pork tenderloin
- Salt to taste
- 1 teaspoon Schezwan pepper
- 1 tablespoon soy sauce
- 1 tablespoon vinegar
- 1 teaspoon hot sauce
- 1 tablespoon oyster sauce
- ¼ teaspoon chili flakes

Directions:
1. Preheat the Ninja Foodi Multi-Cooker at Air Crisp Mode at 390° F for 5 minutes. Use the Ninja Foodi Multi-Cooker function.
2. Combine all the sauces, chili flakes, salt, and pepper in a bowl. Put in the tenderloin and let it rest for 15-20 minutes.
3. Place the tenderloin in the Ninja Foodi Multi-Cooker Basket. Give it an olive oil spray and let it cook at 390° F for 20 minutes. Once the internal temperature reaches 145° F, it's done.
4. Serve pork with cooked brown gravy!

Nutritional Values Per Serving:
Calories: 367; Fat: 9.1g; Carbohydrates: 5.1g ; Protein: 59.9g

Sweet Sour Fish

Prep Time: 10 minutes
Cook Time: 6 minutes
Servings: 4

Ingredients:
- 1-pound fish chunks
- 1 tablespoon vinegar
- 2 drops liquid stevia
- ¼ cup butter
- Black pepper and salt to taste

Directions:
1. Select "Sauté" mode on your Ninja Foodi
2. Stir in butter and melt it
3. Add fish chunks, sauté for 3 minutes
4. Stir in stevia, salt, pepper, stir it
5. Close the crisping lid
6. Cook on "Air Crisp" mode for 3 minutes to 360-degrees F
7. Serve and enjoy.

Nutritional Values Per Serving:
Calories: 274g; Fat: 15g; Carbohydrates: 2g; Protein: 33g

Cajun Shrimp

Prep Time: 10 minutes
Cook Time: 7 minutes
Servings: 4

Ingredients:
- 1 ¼ pound shrimp
- ¼ teaspoon cayenne pepper
- ½ teaspoon old bay seasoning
- ¼ teaspoon smoked paprika
- 1 pinch of salt
- 1 tablespoon olive oil

Directions:
1. Preheat Ninja Foodi by pressing the "AIR CRISP" option and setting it to "390 Degrees F" and timer to 10 minutes
2. Dip the shrimp into a spice mixture and oil
3. Transfer the prepared shrimp to your Ninja Foodi Grill cooking basket and cook for 5 minutes
4. Serve and enjoy.

Nutritional Values Per Serving:
Calories: 170; Fat: 2g; Carbohydrates: 5g; Protein: 23g

Panko Crusted Cod

Prep Time: 10 minutes
Cook Time: 15 minutes
Servings: 4

Ingredients:
- 2 uncooked cod fillets
- 3 teaspoons kosher salt
- ¾ cup panko bread crumbs
- 2 tablespoons butter, melted
- ¼ cup fresh parsley, minced
- 1 lemon. Zested and juiced

Directions:
1. Pre-heat your Ninja Foodi at 390 degrees F and place the Air Crisper basket inside
2. Season cod and salt
3. Take a suitable and stir in bread crumbs, parsley, lemon juice, zest, butter, and mix well
4. Coat fillets with the bread crumbs mixture and place fillets in your Air Crisping basket
5. Lock Crisping lid and cook on Air Crisp mode for 15 minutes at 360 degrees F
6. Serve and enjoy.

Nutritional Values Per Serving:
Calories: 554; Fat: 24g; Carbohydrates: 5g; Protein: 37g

Buttery Scallops

Prep Time: 18 minutes
Cook Time: 6 minutes
Servings: 4

Ingredients:
- 2 pounds sea scallops
- 12 cup butter
- 4 garlic cloves, minced
- 4 tablespoons rosemary, chopped
- Black pepper and salt to taste

Directions:
1. Select "Sauté" mode on your Ninja Foodi on Medium-High heat.
2. Add rosemary, garlic and butter, Sauté for 1 minute
3. Stir in scallops, Black pepper and salt, Sauté for 2 minutes.
4. Close the crisping lid.
5. Cook for 3 minutes.
6. Serve and enjoy.

Nutritional Values Per Serving:
Calories: 278g; Fat: 15g; Carbohydrates: 5g; Protein: 25g

Ninja Foodi Salmon Soup

Prep Time: 15 minutes
Cook Time: 24 minutes
Servings: 10

Ingredients:

- 2 pounds boneless salmon, cubed
- 2 tablespoons olive oil
- 8 cups chicken broth
- 2 tablespoons tamari
- Salt and black pepper, to taste

Directions:
1. Add oil and salmon in a large Ninja Foodi Multi-cooker, sauté for about 5 minutes and press the "Broil" button.
2. Stir in broth and close the Crisping Lid.
3. Press the "Start/Stop" button and boil the mixture for about 15 minutes.
4. Open the lid and add in salt, pepper and tamari.
5. Cook for 4 minutes and take out.
6. Serve and enjoy!

Nutritional Values Per Serving:
Calories: 88; Fat: 5.3g; Carbohydrates: 0.9g; Protein: 8.9g

Salmon Kale Meal

Prep Time: 16 minutes
Cook Time: 4 minutes
Servings: 4

Ingredients:
- 1 lemon, juiced
- 2 salmon fillets
- ¼ cup extra virgin olive oil
- 1 teaspoon Dijon mustard
- 4 cups kale, sliced, ribs removed
- 1 teaspoon salt
- 1 avocado, diced
- 1 cup pomegranate seeds
- 1 cup walnuts, toasted
- 1 cup goat parmesan cheese, shredded

Directions:
1. Season salmon with salt and keep it on the side
2. Place a rack in your Ninja Foodi
3. Place salmon over the rack.
4. Release pressure naturally over 10 minutes
5. Transfer salmon to a serving platter
6. Take a suitable and stir in kale, season with salt
7. Season kale with dressing and add diced avocado, pomegranate seeds, walnuts and cheese
8. Toss and serve with the fish
9. Enjoy.

Nutritional Values Per Serving:
Calories: 234; Fat: 14g; Carbohydrates: 12g; Protein: 16g

Ninja Foodi Squid Rings

Prep Time: 10 minutes
Cook Time: 13 minutes
Servings: 6

Ingredients:
- ½ onion, sliced
- 2 pounds squid, cut into rings
- 2 teaspoons extra-virgin olive oil
- 2 eggs, beaten
- Salt and black pepper, to taste

Directions:
1. Add oil and onion in a Ninja Foodi Multi-cooker and select "Pressure".
2. Press the "Start/Stop" button and sauté for about 5 minutes.
3. Add in squid rings, salt and pepper. Toss to coat well.
4. Simmer for about 5-minutes and stir in eggs.
5. Close the pressure Lid and cook for about 3 minutes at HIGH pressure.
6. Take out, serve and enjoy!

Nutritional Values Per Serving:
Calories: 177; Fat: 5.1g; Carbohydrates: 5.6g; Protein: 25.5g

Ninja Foodi Stir-Fried Shrimp

Prep Time: 5 minutes
Cook Time: 6 minutes
Servings: 6

Ingredients:
- 2 pounds shrimp, peeled and deveined
- 8 tablespoons tamari
- 8 garlic cloves, minced
- 2 tablespoons olive oil
- Salt and black pepper, to taste

Directions:
1. Add oil in Ninja Foodi Multi-cooker and sauté garlic in it for about 1 minute.
2. Stir in shrimp, salt, tamari and black pepper and close the pressure Lid.
3. Select "Pressure" and press the "Start/Stop" button.
4. Cook for about 5 minutes at HIGH pressure and open the lid.
5. Take out, serve and enjoy!

Nutritional Values Per Serving:
Calories: 240; Fat: 7.3g; Carbohydrates: 5g; Protein: 37.2g

Ninja Foodi Rosemary Scallops

Prep Time: 10 minutes
Cook Time: 8 minutes
Servings: 6

Ingredients:
- 2 pounds sea scallops
- 4 tablespoons fresh rosemary, chopped
- 4 tablespoons extra-virgin olive oil
- 4 garlic cloves, minced
- Salt and black pepper, to taste

Directions:
1. Add olive oil, rosemary and garlic in the pot of Ninja Foodi Multi-cooker, sauté for about 2 minutes and select "Sear".
2. Stir in scallops, salt and pepper and close the pressure Lid.
3. Press the "Start/Stop" button and cook for about 3 minutes on each side.
4. Open the lid and take out.
5. Serve and enjoy!

Nutritional Values Per Serving:
Calories: 223; Fat: 10.8g; Carbohydrates: 5.7g; Protein: 25.6g

Ninja Foodi Parsley Baked Salmon

Prep Time: 10 minutes
Cook Time: 20 minutes
Servings: 3

Ingredients:
- 1 pound salmon fillets
- ¾ tablespoon olive oil
- 1½ tablespoons fresh parsley, minced
- ¼ teaspoon ginger powder
- Salt and black pepper, to taste

Directions:
1. Place salmon fillets in Ninja Foodi Multi-cooker and top them with olive oil, parsley, ginger powder, salt and pepper.
2. Press the "Bake" button and close the Crisping Lid.
3. Press the "Start/Stop" button and bake for 20 minutes at 400 degrees F.
4. Open the lid and take out.
5. Serve and enjoy!

Nutritional Values Per Serving:
Calories: 233; Fat: 12.9g; Carbohydrates: 0.6g; Protein: 29.6g

Ninja Foodi Broiled Mahi-Mahi

Prep Time: 10 minutes
Cook Time: 10 minutes
Servings: 2

Ingredients:
- ½ pound mahi-mahi fillets
- ½ tablespoon olive oil

- 2 tablespoon fresh orange juice
- ½ teaspoon dried thyme
- ½ teaspoon cayenne pepper
- Salt and black pepper, to taste

Directions:
1. Add everything except mahi-mahi fillets in a large bowl and mix well.
2. Stir in mahi-mahi and toss to coat well.
3. Set aside the mixture for about half an hour and remove the fillets from the bowl.
4. Place them in Ninja Foodi Multi-cooker and press the "Broil" button.
5. Close the Crisping Lid and press the "Start/Stop" button.
6. Broil for about 10 minutes and open the lid.
7. Dish out and serve hot.

Nutritional Values Per Serving:
Calories: 130; Fat: 3.6g; Carbohydrates: 2.1g; Protein: 21.3g

Ninja Foodi Roasted Tilapia

Prep Time: 10 minutes
Cook Time: 6 minutes
Servings: 2

Ingredients:
- ½ pound tilapia
- ½ tablespoon fresh lime juice
- ¼ tablespoon red pepper flakes
- ½ tablespoon olive oil
- ½ teaspoon black pepper
- Salt, to taste

Directions:
1. Add everything except tilapia fillets in a large bowl. Mix well.
2. Add in tilapia, toss to coat well and set aside for about half an hour.
3. Place marinated tilapia fillets the pot of Ninja Foodi Multi-cooker and select "Roast".
4. Close the Crisping Lid and press the "Start/Stop" button.
5. Roast for about 3-minutes per side and open the lid.
6. Take out, serve and enjoy!

Nutritional Values Per Serving:
Calories: 130; Fat: 4.7g; Carbohydrates: 1.6g; Protein: 21.3g

Ninja Foodi Salmon

Prep Time: 5-6 Minutes
Cook Time: 4-5 Minutes
Servings: 4

Ingredients:
- 2 salmon fillets
- 1 cup water
- Juice from 1 lemon, about ½ cup
- Lemon slices
- 4-5 sprigs of fresh dill (or rosemary)
- Salt and pepper to taste

Directions:
1. Pour water and lemon juice into the Ninja Foodi Multi-Cooker.
2. Add lemon slices and dill.
3. Add the fillets.
4. Add the lemon slices on top of the salmon.
5. Sprinkle with salt and pepper.
6. Secure the Ninja Foodi Multi-Cooker Pressure Lid.
7. Make sure the valve is set to Seal, use the manual settings and cook on High Pressure for 4 minutes. Add an additional minute if the fillet is frozen.
8. Once done, release the valve to Vent (quick release) and then open the lid.
9. Serve the salmon immediately or store in fridge.

Nutritional Values Per Serving:
Calories: 273; Fat: 14g; Carbohydrates: 10g; Protein: 25g

Instant Catfish Fillet

Prep Time: 4-5 Minutes
Cook Time: 15-20 Minutes
Servings: 1

Ingredients:
- 3-4 Catfish fillets
- ½ cup fish fry
- Olive oil spray

Directions:
1. Now evenly coat each catfish fillet with fish fry.
2. Place it in at Air Crisp Mode of Ninja Foodi Multi-Cooker and give it an oil spray. Let it cook for 10 minutes at 390° F.
3. Flip the catfish, give another oil spray and cook for another 10 minutes and serve it!

Nutritional Values Per Serving:
Calories: 266; Fat: 3.4g; Carbohydrates: 28g; Protein: 27g

Ninja Foodi Air Crisp Herbed Salmon

Prep Time: 1 Minutes
Cook Time: 4-5 Minutes
Servings: 6

Ingredients:
- 8 ounces sizzle fish salmon fillets, I used two, 4 ounces sizzle fish sockeye salmon fillets
- 1 teaspoon Herbes de Provence
- ¼ teaspoon natural ancient sea salt
- ¼ teaspoon black pepper
- ¼ teaspoon smoked paprika
- 2 tablespoon olive oil
- 1 tablespoon Medlee Seasoned Butter

Directions:
1. Dry your filets with a paper towel and run the surface gently to ensure that there are no bones
2. Drizzle the olive oil on the fish and rub it in on both sides of the fish.
3. Mix the seasonings and sprinkle them on both sides of the fish.
4. Turn your Air Crisp on 390° F and set Timer for five to 8 minutes and cook. I recommend starting with 5 minutes, checking the fish, and increasing the time by one additional minute until it flakes easily with a fork.
5. Melt the seasoned butter for 30 seconds in the microwave and pour it over the fish before eating.

Nutritional Values Per Serving:
Calories: 338; Fat: 27g; Carbohydrates 1g; Protein: 23g

Ninja Foodi Ginger Cod

Prep Time: 10 minutes
Cook Time: 20 minutes
Servings: 2

Ingredients:
- ½ pound cod fillets
- 1 tablespoon fresh lime juice
- ½ tablespoon fresh ginger, minced
- 1 tablespoon coconut aminos
- Salt and black pepper, to taste

Directions:
1. Add lime juice, fresh ginger, coconut aminos, salt and pepper in a bowl. Mix well.
2. Add cod fillets in the mixture and toss to coat well.
3. Place them in the pot of Ninja Foodi Multi-cooker and press the "Bake" button.
4. Close the Crisping Lid and press the "Start/Stop" button.
5. Bake for about 20-minutes at 325 degrees F and open the lid.
6. Take out, serve and enjoy!

Nutritional Values Per Serving:
Calories: 109; Fat: 1.1g; Carbohydrates: 4.3g; Protein: 20.5g

Spicy Shrimps

Prep Time: 8-10 Minutes
Cook Time: 12-15 Minutes
Servings: 2

Ingredients:
- 1 pound shrimps
- Salt to taste
- Pepper to taste
- ½ teaspoon cumin powder
- 1 teaspoon coriander powder
- ½ teaspoon red chili powder
- 1 tablespoon lemon juice
- 1 cup mixed vegetables
- Foil (3 to 4 sheets)
- Cooking oil spray (olive or coconut)

Directions:
1. Spray the foil sheets with olive oil. Do this on about a maximum of four sheets.
2. Season it up with salt, pepper, red chili padder, cumin, and coriander powder. Pour in some lemon juice and coat all the shrimps well.
3. Again, spray another coat of olive oil on foil sheets and put the shrimps on the foil.
4. Using the Bake function, preheat the Ninja Foodi Multi-Cooker at 375° F.
5. Cook it using a Bake function at 375° F for 13 to 15 minutes. Do this by placing foil sheets in it.

Nutritional Values Per Serving:
Calories: 188; Fat: 10g; Carbohydrates: 10.1g; Protein: 37.3g

Ninja Foodi Salmon with Sweet Potatoes

Prep Time: 10 minutes
Cook Time: 9 hours
Servings: 3

Ingredients:
- ½ pound salmon fillets, cubed
- ¾ cup chicken broth
- ¼ teaspoon ground nutmeg
- 2 sweet potatoes, sliced thinly
- ½ onion, chopped
- Salt and black pepper, to taste

Directions:
1. Place half of the sweetpotatoes in the bottom of the Ninja Foodi Multi-cooker and season them with salt and pepper.
2. Place salmon fillets and onion on the top and sprinkle ground nutmeg on it.
3. Then, top with remaining sweet potato slices and close the pressure Lid.
4. Select "Slow Cook" and press the "Start/Stop" button.
5. Cook for about 9 hours at LOW TEMP and open the lid.
6. Take out, serve and enjoy!

Nutritional Values Per Serving:
Calories: 236; Fat: 5.3g; Carbohydrates: 29.9g; Protein: 17.6g

Mixed Seafood Platter

Prep Time: 9 Minutes
Cook Time: 6 Minutes
Servings: 6

Ingredients:
- 1 pound peeled and devein fresh shrimps
- 1 pound mussels
- 1 potato (coarsely cut)
- ½ cup fresh corn
- 340 g of sausage (2-inch pieces)
- 2-3 cups water
- 2 tablespoons old bay seasoning
- 2 teaspoons oil flakes
- ¼ cup fresh chopped parsley
- Butter melted 1 cup
- Garlic powder 1 tsp

Directions:
1. Add potatoes, corn, sausages, water, and oil flakes in the Ninja Foodi Multi-Cooker Pot. Give it a good stir.
2. Now on the High Pressure, cook it for 4 minutes and do a quick release.
3. Once the one-timer is completed and pressure is released, open the lid carefully.
4. Now add shrimps and mussels and old bay seasoning. Mix it well and cook it on High Pressure setting in Ninja Foodi Multi-Cooker for 1 minute. Allow for natural release of pressure for 2 minutes, after 1 minute of cooking

in Ninja Foodi Multi-Cooker High Pressure setting.
5. Then add butter and garlic powder to a small bowl. Mix it well and top up with parsley. Drizzle all over the platter.

Nutritional Values Per Serving:
Calories: 521; Fat: 39.9g; Carbohydrates: 22.6g; Protein: 19.3g

Beer Battered Fish

Prep Time: 8-10 Minutes
Cook Time: 12-15 Minutes
Servings: 4

Ingredients:
- 1 pound codfish cuts
- 1 cup flour
- ½ teaspoon baking soda
- 2 tablespoons Cornstarch
- 4 ounces beer
- 1 beaten egg
- Salt as required
- ¼ teaspoon Cayenne pepper
- 1 tablespoon olive oil

For Flour Mix
- ¾ cup of flour
- 1 teaspoon paprika powder
- ½ teaspoon black pepper

Directions:
1. Combine flour, cornstarch, salt, cayenne pepper, and baking soda in a large bowl. Then add egg and beer, and stir it until it becomes a smooth batter. Let it refrigerate for 20 minutes.
2. Take ¾ cup of flour, paprika, black pepper in a shallow pan.

3. The fish should be at least one half-inch thick so that it does not dry out in the Ninja Foodi Multi-Cooker Cook & Crisp Basket. Take a paper towel and pat dry the codfish cuts.
4. Now coat all sides while dipping the fish into the batter.
5. Allow the eggs batter to dip off and again coat it with seasoned flour mix. Any leftover flour can be sprinkled on the fish fillet.
6. Now preheat the Ninja Foodi Multi-Cooker at Air Crisp Mode at 390° F for 5 minutes. Spray both sides of the coated fish fillet with vegetable oil and then place them in the Ninja Foodi Multi-Cooker Cook & Crisp Basket for 12 minutes.
7. During the cooking process, add a little more oil if there is any dryness in the coating!

Nutritional Values Per Serving:
Calories: 407; Fat: 6g; Carbohydrates: 26.6g; Protein: 7.3g

Gluten-free fish tacos

Prep Time: 8 Minutes
Cook Time: 15-17 Minutes
Servings: 6

Ingredients:
- 4 fish fillets
- 1 teaspoon paprika powder
- ½ teaspoon salt and pepper
- 1 teaspoon mixed herbs
- 6-8 tortillas wrap

For Corn Salsa:
- 1 cup soft-cooked corn
- 1 cup tomatoes
- ½ cup onion
- ½ cup chopped coriander
- 1 tablespoon lemon juice

Directions:
1. Take the thawed fish and place it into the Cook & Crisp Basket, then add paprika, salt, and pepper.
2. Spray the Cook & Crisp Basket with olive oil and put it in the Ninja Foodi Multi-Cooker.
3. Preheat Ninja Foodi Multi-Cooker at Air Crisp Mode at 390° F for 12 minutes.
4. Meanwhile, combine the ingredients in a bowl for corn salsa. Squeeze a lemon juice on top of corn salsa then remove and flake it apart with a fork once the fish is cooked fully.
5. Now place each tortilla on a plate and add fish and then top it with the corn salsa. Now

place each tortilla next to each other in the Ninja Foodi Multi-Cooker Cook & Crisp Basket.
6. Give it a cooking spray, for 5 minutes Air Crisp it at 390° F with tongs, remove it carefully, and serve it.

Nutritional Values Per Serving:
Calories: 294; Fat: 7.3g; Carbohydrates: 49.2g; Protein: 7g

Lobster Tail

Prep Time: 4 Minutes
Cook Time: 6 Minutes
Servings: 2

Ingredients:
- 4 lobster tails
- 4 tablespoons butter (unsalted)
- 2 crushed garlic cloves
- 1 tablespoon mixed dried herbs
- 1 teaspoon Slash parsley
- Salt and pepper to taste

Directions:
1. Preheat the Ninja Foodi Multi-Cooker at 375° F for the Bake function by setting the Bake Mode for 5 minutes.
2. Meanwhile, cut the lobster using kitchen scissors then cut the center of the tail until you reach the fins. Do not cut them. Use your fingers to bring the meat up to the top by pulling apart the tail and closing the shell.
3. It should create a butterfly with the meat when you're cutting it so that it can easily be moved to the top of the shell.
4. Melt the butter, add garlic and parsley and mix well in a small bowl. Now drench the lobster tails in a butter mixture.
5. Now place the lobster tail in the Ninja Foodi Multi-Cooker Cook & Crisp Basket very carefully, and spray olive oil generously.
6. For 5 minutes cook the lobsters, or until the internal temperature of the meat reaches at least 145° F. Lift the lid of the Ninja Foodi Multi-Cooker once it's done.
7. Take out the golden lobsters and serve!

Nutritional Values Per Serving:
Calories: 565; Fat: 36g; Carbohydrates: 0.2g; Protein: 46.3g

Fish Skewers

Prep Time: 3 Minutes
Cook Time: 8-10 Minutes
Servings: 4

Ingredients:
- 1 pound frozen fish cubes
- 6-8 skewers
- Salt to taste
- Pepper to taste
- 2 tablespoon ginger garlic paste
- ½ teaspoon paprika
- 1 tablespoon lemon juice
- 1 teaspoon oregano
- ½ teaspoon liquid charcoal
- 1 tablespoon olive oil

Directions:
1. Oil spray the Ninja Foodi Multi-Cooker Cook & Crisp Basket. Combine the fish cubes with all the seasonings in a bowl. Set aside for one to two hours.
2. Align the cubes on the skewers. Now place the fish sticks in an even manner into the Ninja Foodi Multi-Cooker Basket.
3. For 10 minutes, cook at 390° F in Air Crisp Mode. Flip it if needed and the skewers are ready to be served!

Nutritional Values Per Serving:
Calories: 182; Fat: 8.5g; Carbohydrates: 3g; Protein: 23.3g

Crumbed Tilapia

Prep Time: 12 Minutes

Cook Time: 6 Minutes
Servings: 4

Ingredients:
- 4 frozen tilapia fillets
- 1 cup bread crumbs
- 2 tbsp seafood seasoning
- 1 egg
- Olive oil spray

Directions:
1. At 390° F, preheat the Ninja Foodi Multi-Cooker at Air Crisp Mode for 5 minutes.
2. To pat dry the fillet, use paper towels and dry the moisture.
3. Add salt and pepper to the egg in a bowl and whisk it well. First, dip the fillet in the whisked egg.
4. Combine bread crumbs with seafood seasoning on a plate and press the fillet from both sides into that mixture to coat generously.
5. Place the fillets in the Ninja Foodi Multi-Cooker Cook & Crisp Basket and close the lid and cook depending on the thickness of the tilapia and in most cases, 4 minutes have been a good amount of time for a good result. Take out the golden crispy fillets and eat a proteinaceous meal!

Nutritional Values Per Serving:
Calories: 212; Fat: 4.5g; Carbohydrates: 15.9g; Protein: 27.5g

Lemon Garlic Scallops

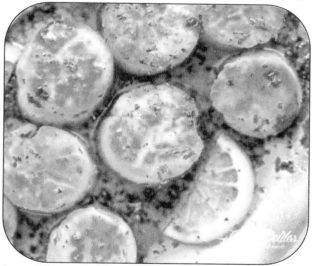

Prep Time: 8-10 Minutes
Cook Time: 15-20 Minutes
Servings: 2

Ingredients
- 1 pound scallops
- ½ teaspoon pepper
- ½ teaspoon salt
- 1 tablespoon extra-virgin olive oil
- 2 tablespoons chopped parsley
- ¼ teaspoon lemon zest
- 1 teaspoon chopped garlic

Directions:

1. Season scallops with pepper and salt. Give the Ninja Foodi Multi-Cooker Cook & Crisp Basket a generous oil spray.
2. Set the Ninja Foodi Multi-Cooker at Air Crisp at 390° F, cook the scallops for about 6 minutes.
3. Now take a small bowl and add oil, parsley, lemon zest, and garlic.
4. Once scallops are seared well, drizzle this mixture over the scallops!

Nutritional Values Per Serving:
Calories: 320; Fat: 10.2g; Carbohydrates: 14.4g; Protein: 35.4g

Ninja Foodi Asparagus Scallops

Prep Time: 10 minutes
Cook Time: 10 minutes
Servings: 8

Ingredients:
- 1½ pounds scallops
- 2 tablespoons coconut oil
- 2 teaspoons lemon zest, finely grated
- ¼ cup shallots, chopped
- 1½ pounds asparagus, chopped
- 2 garlic cloves, minced
- 2 tablespoons fresh lemon juice
- 2 tablespoons fresh rosemary, chopped
- Salt and black pepper, to taste

Directions:
1. Add oil in Ninja Foodi Multi-cooker and sauté shallots in it for about 2 minutes.
2. Select "Sear" and press the "Start/Stop" button.
3. Add in garlic and rosemary and Sauté for about 1 minute.
4. Stir in asparagus and lemon zest and cook for about 2 minutes.

5. Add in scallops, lemon juice, salt and pepper and cook for about 5 minutes.
6. Take out and serve hot.

Nutritional Values Per Serving:
Calories: 375; Fat: 6.3g; Carbohydrates: 21.3g; Protein: 59.5g

Ninja Foodi Ginger Salmon

Prep Time: 10 minutes
Cook Time: 18 minutes
Servings: 3

Ingredients:
- ¼ pound salmon fillets
- ½ teaspoon fresh ginger, minced
- ½ tablespoon sesame seeds
- ½ tablespoon coconut aminos
- ½ tablespoon fresh lime juice
- Salt and black pepper, to taste

Directions:
1. Add all the ingredients to a large bowl and mix well.
2. Dredge salmon fillets in the mixture and transfer them to the pot of Ninja Foodi Multi-cooker.
3. Press the "Bake" button and close the Crisping Lid.
4. Press the "Start/Stop" button and bake for about 18 minutes at 325 degrees F.
5. Open the Crisping Lid and take out.
6. Serve and enjoy!

Nutritional Values Per Serving:
Calories: 64; Fat: 3.1g; Carbohydrates: 1.7g; Protein: 7.7g

Hawaiian Fried Rice

Prep Time: 6 Minutes
Cook Time: 12-15 Minutes
Servings: 3-4

Ingredients:
- ½ cup rice
- 1 cup water
- 1 tablespoon cooking oil
- ½ cup frozen peas
- ½ cup corn
- ½ cup diced carrots
- 1 tablespoon soya sauce
- ¼ cup chopped green onions
- 1 scrambled egg
- 1 cup shredded chicken
- Salt according to taste

Directions:
1. Combine rice, water, and oil in the inner pot of the Ninja Foodi Multi-Cooker.
2. Set on High pressure for 1 minute and put the pressure lid on and set the back of the valve to Seal. Release the pressure immediately.
3. Cut the vegetables while the rice is being cooked. Then except for the eggs and green onions, add all the remaining ingredients.
4. Put on the Ninja Foodi Multi-Cooker Crispy lid and set to 390° F, set the Ninja Foodi Multi-Cooker to Air Crisp Mode Timer for 10 minutes, and keep stirring occasionally.
5. Make a well in the center pushing the rice to the edges, pour the egg, and scramble it.
6. Turn on the Ninja Foodi Multi-Cooker Mode at Medium temperature on High and add the green onion to it. Cook it for 2 to 3 minutes and dish out the refreshing rice!

Nutrition Information per Serving:
Calories: 187; Fat: 10.5g; Carbohydrates: 14.6g; Protein: 9.3.

Ninja Foodi Cauliflower Fried Rice

Prep Time: 10 minutes
Cook Time: 15 minutes
Servings: 4

Ingredients:
- 4 cups riced cauliflower
- ¼ cup diced green onion
- ½ teaspoon garlic powder
- ½ teaspoon ground ginger
- 2 tablespoons low-sodium soy sauce
- 1 egg, beaten
- ½ cup peas
- ¼ cup shredded carrots
- 2 tablespoons olive oil

Directions:
1. Add olive oil in Ninja Foodi Multi-cooker. Select to sauté mode.
2. Press the "Start/Stop" button and sauté peas, carrot and onion in it.
3. Add in egg, garlic powder, and ginger. Stir properly.
4. Stir in cauliflower rice and close the pressure Lid.
5. Cook for about 5 minutes and open the lid.
6. Add in soy sauce and mix well.
7. Take out, serve and enjoy!

Nutritional Values Per Serving:
Calories: 130; Fat: 8.2g; Carbohydrates: 9.8g; Protein: 5.1g

Cauliflower chunks with Lemon Sauce

Prep Time: 5 minutes
Cook Time: 15 minutes
Servings: 4

Ingredients:
- 1-pound cauliflower, cut into chunks
- 1 tablespoon dill, chopped
- 1 tablespoon lemon zest, grated
- Juice of ½ lemon
- 2 tablespoons butter, melted
- Black pepper and salt to the taste

Directions:
1. Set the Foodi on Sauté mode, stir in the butter, melt it, add the cauliflower chunks and brown for 5 minutes.
2. Add the lemon zest and the other ingredients set the machine on Air Crisp and cook at 390 degrees F for 10 minutes.
3. Divide everything between plates and serve.

Nutritional Values Per Serving:
Calories: 122; Fat: 3.3g; Carbohydrates: 3g; Protein: 2g

Radish Apples Salad

Prep Time: 5 minutes
Cook Time: 15 minutes
Servings: 4

Ingredients:
- 1-pound radishes, roughly cubed

- 2 apples, cored and cut into wedges
- ¼ cup chicken stock
- 2 spring onions, chopped
- 3 tablespoons tomato paste
- Juice of 1 lime
- Cooking spray
- 1 tablespoon cilantro, chopped

Directions:
1. In your Ninja Foodi, combine the radishes with the apples and the other ingredients
2. Put the Ninja Foodi's lid on and cook on High for 15 minutes.
3. Release the pressure quickly for 5 minutes, divide everything between plates and serve.

Nutritional Values Per Serving:
Calories: 122; Fat: 5g; Carbohydrates: 4.5g; Protein: 3g

Balsamic Cabbage with Endives

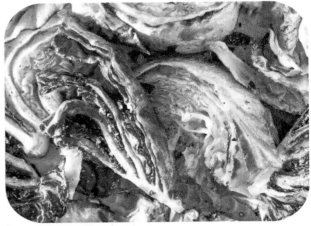

Prep Time: 5 minutes
Cook Time: 15 minutes
Servings: 4

Ingredients:
- 1 green cabbage head, shredded
- 2 endives, trimmed and sliced lengthwise
- Black pepper and salt to the taste
- 1 tablespoon olive oil
- 2 shallots, chopped
- ½ cup chicken stock
- 1 tablespoon sweet paprika
- 1 tablespoon balsamic vinegar

Directions:
1. Set the Foodi on Sauté mode, stir in the oil, heat it up, add the shallots and sauté for 2 minutes.
2. Add the cabbage, the endives and the other ingredients.
3. Put the Ninja Foodi's lid on and cook on High for 13 minutes.
4. Release the pressure quickly for 5 minutes, divide the mix between plates and serve.

Nutritional Values Per Serving:
Calories: 120; Fat: 2g; Carbohydrates: 3.3g; Protein: 4

Veggie Pot Pie

Prep Time: 8-10 Minutes
Cook Time: 20-25 Minutes
Servings: 4

Ingredients:
- 2 tablespoon butter
- 1 small onion
- 1 cup diced carrots
- 1 teaspoon ginger garlic paste
- ½ cup sliced potatoes
- ½ cup vegetable broth.
- ⅛ cup pie
- 4 tablespoons corn
- 1 tablespoon parsley
- 2 tablespoon flour
- ½ cup cream
- Salt to taste
- Pepper to taste
- Pie crust (pre-prepared)

Directions:
1. Start the Ninja Foodi Multi-Cooker and set to Medium-High temperature, then press the Start/Stop button and let the Ninja Foodi Multi-Cooker Pot preheat. It would take about 5 minutes. Now put melted butter in the pot. Add carrots, onions in it for about 3 minutes on Sauté Mode.
2. Now add ginger garlic paste to the veggies and cook. Make sure to keep stirring it constantly for about 30 seconds.
3. Then add potatoes and broth to the pot. Put on the Pressure Lid after stirring a little and close the lid to Seal.
4. Now cook on High Pressure Cook Ninja Foodi Multi-Cooker setting for 5 minutes.
5. Do a quick release, when done and remove the lid now. Add the pies, parsley, and corn to the Ninja Foodi Multi-Cooker Pot. Then put in flour and mix well. Then stir in cream (heavy cream is preferred) and give it a good mix.
6. Select Sear, and set to High temperature, press Start/Stop to cook it and keep stirring it constantly, until the sauce thickens up, do this for 2 to 3 minutes, and then press the Start/Stop button.
7. Add in salt and pepper to season. Now comes the interesting part, place the pie crust on top of the vegetable mixture and hold the edges of the crust to fit the Ninja Foodi Multi-Cooker Pot.
8. Make a little vent in the center of the crust, now close the Crisping Lid and select the Broil Mode, set the timer for about 10 minutes, and press the Start/Stop button.
9. Transfer the Ninja Foodi Multi-Cooker Inner Pot to any heatproof surface, after time is up. Let it sit for about four to 5 minutes and it's ready to be served!

Nutritional Values Per Serving:
Calories: 404; Fat: 22.5g; Carbohydrates: 19.4g; Protein: 4g

Air Crisped Brussels Sprouts

Prep Time: 6 Minutes
Cook Time: 12-15 Minutes
Servings: 2-3

Ingredients:
- ¼ pound brussels sprouts
- 2 slices of bacon
- 1 onion
- Salt to taste
- Pepper to taste

Directions:
1. Preheat the Ninja Foodi Multi-Cooker by selecting Air Crisp Mode at 390° F for about 5 minutes.
2. Cut off the ends of brussels sprouts and slice them in half. Cut the bacon into small pieces and cut the onions into slices.
3. Put all the ingredients including brussels sprouts, onions, and bacon in Ninja Foodi Multi-Cooker.
4. Season it with salt and pepper. Let it cook for 15 minutes and mix occasionally. Keep a check and make sure it does not burn!

Nutritional Values Per Serving:
Calories: 90; Fat: 2.3g; Carbohydrates: 14.5g; Protein: 7.1g

Maple Dipped Kale

Prep Time: 5 minutes
Cook Time: 15 minutes
Servings: 4

Ingredients:
- 2 pounds kale, torn
- ½ cup soy sauce
- 1 teaspoon choc zero maple syrup
- 2 teaspoons olive oil
- ½ teaspoon garlic powder
- Black pepper and salt

Directions:
1. In your Ninja Foodi, combine the kale with the soy sauce and the other ingredients.
2. Put the Ninja Foodi's lid on and cook on High for 15 minutes.
3. Release the pressure quickly for 5 minutes, divide everything between plates and serve.

Nutritional Values Per Serving:
Calories: 120; Fat: 3.5g; Carbohydrates: 3.3g; Protein: 1.1g

Ninja Foodi Spinach and Onion Soup

Prep Time: 10 minutes
Cook Time: 20 minutes
Servings: 6

Ingredients:
- 4 chicken bouillon cubes
- 6 celery stalks, chopped
- ½ cup spinach, chopped
- ½ cup chopped onion
- 1 cup water
- Salt and black pepper, to taste

Directions:
1. Add water and chicken bouillon cubes in the pot of Ninja Foodi Multi-cooker and press the "Broil" button.
2. Close the Crisping Lid and press the "Start/Stop" button.
3. Cook for about 5 minutes and open the lid.
4. Stir in vegetables and simmer the mixture for 15 minutes.
5. Take out, serve and enjoy!

Nutritional Values Per Serving:
Calories: 13; Fat: 0.3g; Carbohydrates: 2.1g; Protein: 0.7g

Ninja Foodi Asparagus Soup

Prep Time: 10 minutes
Cook Time: 40 minutes
Servings: 3

Ingredients:
- 1 pound asparagus, chopped
- 3 cups vegetable broth
- 1½ tablespoons lemon juice
- 2 scallions, chopped
- 1 tablespoon olive oil
- Salt and black pepper, to taste

Directions:
1. Heat oil in Ninja Foodi Multi-cooker and select "Pressure".
2. Sauté scallions in it for about 5 minutes and stir in broth and asparagus.
3. Cook for about 5 minutes and let the mixture simmer for about 25 minutes.
4. Take out, place it in a food-processor and pulse to form a smooth mixture.
5. Pour it again in the pot of Ninja Foodi Multi-cooker and close the lid.
6. Select "pressure" and press the "Start/Stop" button.
7. Cook for 5 minutes at HIGH pressure and open the lid.
8. Stir in salt, lemon juice and pepper and take out.
9. Serve hot and enjoy!

Nutritional Values Per Serving:
Calories: 119; Fat: 6.5g; Carbohydrates: 8.1g; Protein: 8.6g

Ninja Foodi Broccoli Soup

Prep Time: 15 minutes
Cook Time: 40 minutes
Servings: 6

Ingredients:
- 2 broccoli, cut into florets
- 1½ garlic cloves, minced
- ¼ tablespoons red pepper flakes, crushed
- ½ cup chopped onion
- 6 cups vegetable broth
- 1½ tablespoons chopped thyme
- ¼ teaspoon ground cumin

Directions:
1. Heat half cup vegetable broth in Ninja Foodi Multi-cooker and press the "Broil" button.
2. Sauté onion in it and add in garlic, thyme, cumin and red pepper flakes after 5 minutes. Mix well.
3. Sauté for 1 minute and stir in half cup broth and broccoli.
4. Cook for about 4 minutes and stir in remaining the broth.
5. Close the Crisping Lid and simmer the mixture for half an hour.
6. Open the lid and take out.
7. Pour it in the blender and blend until a smooth mixture is formed.
8. Take out, serve and enjoy!

Nutritional Values Per Serving:
Calories: 65; Fat: 1.7g; Carbohydrates: 6.5g; Protein: 6.3g

Ninja Foodi Vegetables Smoothie

Prep Time: 10 minutes
Cook Time: 5 minutes
Servings: 4

Ingredients:
- ½ cup chopped spinach
- 1 cup broccoli florets, chopped
- 1 cup chopped green bell peppers
- 3 cups chilled water
- 1 cup green cabbage, chopped
- 2 teaspoons sugar

Directions:
1. Add spinach, broccoli, bell peppers, cabbage, sugar and water in the pot of Ninja Foodi Multi-cooker.
2. Select "Pressure" and close the pressure Lid.
3. Press the "Start/Stop" button and cook for 5 minutes at LOW pressure.
4. Open the lid, take out and refrigerate for 2 to 3 hours.
5. Pour in serving glasses and serve.

Nutritional Values Per Serving:
Calories: 30; Fat: 0.2g; Carbohydrates: 6.9g; Protein: 1.3g

Cabbage with Bacon

Prep Time: 5 minutes
Cook Time: 20 minutes
Servings: 4

Ingredients:
- 4 cups red cabbage, shredded
- ¼ cup veggie stock
- A pinch of black pepper and salt
- 1 tablespoon olive oil
- 1 cup canned tomatoes, crushed
- Zest of 1 lime, grated
- 2 ounces bacon, cooked and crumbled

Directions:
1. Put the reversible rack in the Foodi, add the baking pan inside and grease it with the oil.
2. Add the cabbage, the stock and the other ingredients into the pan.
3. Cook on Baking mode at 380 degrees F for 20 minutes.
4. Divide the mix between plates and serve.

Nutritional Values Per Serving:
Calories: 144; Fat: 3g; Carbohydrates: 4.5g; Protein: 4.4g

Cabbage with Carrots

Prep Time: 5 minutes
Cook Time: 20 minutes
Servings: 4

Ingredients:
- 1 Napa cabbage, shredded
- 2 carrots, sliced
- 2 tablespoons olive oil
- 1 red onion, chopped
- Black pepper and salt to the taste
- 2 tablespoons sweet paprika
- ½ cup tomato sauce

Directions:
1. Set the Foodi on Sauté mode, stir in the oil, heat it up, add the onion and sauté for 5 minutes.
2. Add the carrots, the cabbage and the other ingredients, toss.
3. Put the Ninja Foodi's lid on and cook on High for 15 minutes.
4. Release the pressure quickly for 5 minutes, divide everything between plates and serve.

Nutritional Values Per Serving:
Calories: 140; Fat: 3.4g; Carbohydrates: 1.2g; Protein: 3.5 g

Saucy Kale

Prep Time: 5 minutes
Cook Time: 15 minutes
Servings: 4

Ingredients:

- 1-pound kale, torn
- 2 leeks, sliced
- 2 tablespoons balsamic vinegar
- 1 tablespoon parsley, chopped
- Black pepper and salt to the taste
- 2 shallots, chopped
- ½ cup tomato sauce

Directions:
1. In your Ninja Foodi, combine the kale with the leeks and the other ingredients.
2. Put the Ninja Foodi's lid on and cook on High for 15 minutes.
3. Release the pressure quickly for 5 minutes, divide the mix between plates and serve.

Nutritional Values Per Serving:
Calories: 100; Fat: 2g; Carbohydrates: 3.4g; Protein: 4g

Bell Peppers Mix

Prep Time: 5 minutes
Cook Time: 16 minutes
Servings: 4

Ingredients:
- 1-pound red bell peppers, cut into wedges
- ½ teaspoon curry powder
- ½ cup tomato sauce
- Black pepper and salt to the taste
- 1 tablespoon olive oil
- 2 garlic cloves, minced
- 1 tablespoon parsley, chopped

Directions:
1. Put the reversible rack in the Foodi, add the baking pan inside and grease it with the oil.
2. Add the peppers, curry powder and the other ingredients except for the parsley, toss a bit and
3. Cook on Baking mode at 380 degrees F for 16 minutes.
4. Divide cooked peppers between plates and serve with the parsley sprinkled on top.

Nutritional Values Per Serving:
Calories: 150; Fat: 3.5g; Carbohydrates: 3.1g; Protein: 1.2g

Ninja Foodi Tomato Olive Salad

Prep Time: 10 minutes
Cook Time: 2 minutes
Servings: 4

Ingredients:
- 4 tablespoons red wine vinegar
- 5 cucumbers, chopped
- ½ red onion, thinly sliced
- 5 tomatoes, chopped
- ½ cup green olives, chopped
- 1 cup black olives, halved

Directions:
1. Add every ingredient in the pot of Ninja Foodi Multi-cooker and select "Steam".
2. Close the pressure Lid and press the "Start/Stop" button.
3. Cook for 2 minutes and open the lid.
4. Take out and toss to coat well.
5. Serve and enjoy!

Nutritional Values Per Serving:
Calories: 133; Fat: 4.5g; Carbohydrates: 23.3g; Protein: 4.3g

Ninja Foodi Roasted Red Pepper Gazpacho

Prep Time: 10 minutes
Cook Time: 5 minutes
Servings: 2

Ingredients:

- 1 cup cherry tomatoes
- 2 roasted red sweet peppers
- ½ red onion, chopped
- 1 garlic clove, minced
- 1 cucumber, chopped
- 2 tablespoons diced mild green chilies
- 1 tablespoon apple cider vinegar
- 1 tablespoon olive oil

Directions:
1. Add everything in a Ninja Foodi Multi-cooker and select "pressure".
2. Close the pressure Lid and press the "Start/Stop" button.
3. Cook for 5 minutes at HIGH pressure and open the lid.
4. Take out, serve and enjoy!

Nutritional Values Per Serving:
Calories: 131; Fat: 7.5g; Carbohydrates: 15.7g; Protein: 2.7g

Ninja Foodi Kale Salad

Prep Time: 10 minutes
Cook Time: 5 minutes
Servings: 4

Ingredients:
- 2 tomatoes, sliced
- 2 tablespoons fresh lemon juice
- 2 red onions, sliced
- 2 scallions, chopped
- 8 cups fresh kale, trimmed and chopped
- 4 tablespoons fresh orange juice

Directions:
1. Add all the ingredients in the pot of Ninja Foodi Multi-cooker and select "Steam".
2. Close the pressure Lid and press the "Start/Stop" button.
3. Cook for 5 minutes and open the lid.
4. Take out and refrigerate for about 8 hours.
5. Serve and enjoy!

Nutritional Values Per Serving:
Calories: 110; Fat: 0.3g; Carbohydrates: 23.9g; Protein: 5.5g

Minty Radishes

Prep Time: 5 minutes
Cook Time: 15 minutes
Servings: 4

Ingredients:
- 1-pound radishes, halved
- black pepper and salt
- 2 tablespoons balsamic vinegar
- 2 tablespoons mint, chopped
- 2 tablespoons olive oil

Directions:
1. In your Ninja Foodi's basket, combine the radishes with the vinegar and the other ingredients, and
2. Cook on Air Crisp at 380 degrees F for 15 minutes.
3. Divide the radishes between plates and serve.

Nutritional Values Per Serving:
Calories: 170; Fat: 4.5g; Carbohydrates: 7.4g; Protein: 4.6g

Beets and Carrots

Prep Time: 5 minutes
Cook Time: 20 minutes
Servings: 4

Ingredients:
- 1-pound beets, peeled and roughly cubed
- 1-pound baby carrots, peeled
- Black pepper and salt to the taste

- 2 tablespoons olive oil
- 1 tablespoon chives, minced

Directions:
1. In a suitable, mix the beets with the carrots and the other ingredients and toss.
2. Put the beets and carrots in the Foodi's basket.
3. Cook on Air Crisp at 390 degrees F for 20 minutes, divide between plates and serve.

Nutritional Values Per Serving:
Calories: 150; Fat: 4.5g; Carbohydrates: 7.3g; Protein: 3.6g

Steak and Veggie Bowl

Prep Time: 6 Minutes
Cook Time: 12-15 Minutes
Servings: 1

Ingredients:
- 2 steak strips
- ½ coarsely cut red bell pepper
- ½ coarsely cut green bell pepper
- ½ coarsely cut summer squash
- 10 sliced olives
- ½ cup diced onion
- 2 tablespoons barbecue sauce
- Salt to taste
- Black pepper to taste
- Olive oil spray

Directions:
1. Start by cutting the steak into smaller chunks. Spray olive oil in the Ninja Foodi Multi-Cooker Cook & Crisp Basket.
2. Now put the steak chunks and cut vegetables in the Ninja Foodi Multi-Cooker Cook & Crisp Basket. Sprinkle salt, pepper, and barbecue sauce evenly and make sure the seasoning is sprinkled generously.
3. Again, spray with olive oil and cook for seven minutes at 375° F on Bake/Roast option. Open the lid carefully and toss the ingredients.
4. Spray some more olive oil and cook for an additional 8 minutes. Serve it in a bowl!

Nutritional Values Per Serving:
Calories: 19.4g; Fat: 5.2g; Carbohydrates: 12g; Protein: 21g.

Sesame Radish

Prep Time: 5 minutes
Cook Time: 15 minutes
Servings: 4

Ingredients:
- 2 leeks, sliced
- ½ pound radishes, sliced
- 2 scallions, chopped
- 2 tablespoons black sesame seeds
- ⅓ cup chicken stock
- 1 tablespoon ginger, grated
- 1 tablespoon chives, minced

Directions:
1. In your Ninja Foodi, combine the leeks with the radishes and the other ingredients.
2. Put the Ninja Foodi's lid on and cook on High for 15 minutes more.
3. Release the pressure quickly for 5 minutes, divide everything between plates and serve.

Nutritional Values Per Serving:
Calories: 112; Fat: 2g; Carbohydrates: 4.2g; Protein: 2g

Kale and Parmesan

Prep Time: 5 minutes
Cook Time: 15 minutes
Servings: 4

Ingredients:
- 1-pound kale, torn
- 2 tablespoons parmesan, grated
- 1 red onion, sliced
- 1 cup bacon, cooked and chopped
- ½ cup chicken stock

- 1 tablespoon olive oil
- A pinch of black pepper and salt
- 1 tablespoon balsamic vinegar

Directions:
1. Set the Foodi on Sauté mode, stir in the oil, heat it up, add the onion and sauté for 2 minutes.
2. Stir in the kale and the other ingredients except the parmesan.
3. Sprinkle the cheese at the end, set the machine on Baking mode.
4. Cook at 380 degrees F for about 12 minutes.
5. Divide everything into bowls and serve.

Nutritional Values Per Serving:
Calories: 130; Fat: 5g; Carbohydrates: 3.4g; Protein: 6g

Carrots Walnuts Salad

Prep Time: 5 minutes
Cook Time: 15 minutes
Servings: 4

Ingredients:
- 4 carrots, roughly shredded
- ½ cup walnuts, sliced
- 3 tablespoons balsamic vinegar
- 1 cup chicken stock
- Black pepper and salt to the taste
- 1 tablespoon olive oil

Directions:
1. In your Ninja Foodi, mix the carrots with the vinegar and the other ingredients except for the walnuts
2. Put the pressure cooking lid on and cook on High for 15 minutes.
3. Release the pressure quickly for 5 minutes, divide the mix between plates and serve with the walnuts sprinkled on top.

Nutritional Values Per Serving:
Calories: 120; Fat: 4.5g; Carbohydrates: 5.3g; Protein: 1.3g

Ninja Foodi Vegetable Curry

Prep Time: 10 minutes
Cook Time: 27 minutes
Servings: 6

Ingredients:
- 1 tablespoon olive oil
- 1 onion, chopped
- 1 teaspoon fresh thyme, chopped
- 3 cups fresh spinach
- 1 pound Brussel sprouts
- 1 cup sliced mushrooms
- Salt and black pepper, to taste

Directions:
1. Heat oil in a Ninja Foodi Multi-cooker and select "pressure".
2. Press the "Start/Stop" button and sauté onion in it for about 4 minutes.
3. Add in garlic and thyme and sauté for about 1 minute.
4. Stir in mushrooms and cook for about 15 minutes.
5. Then, add in Brussel sprouts and spinach and close the pressure lid.
6. Cook for 7 minutes at HIGH pressure and open the lid.
7. Stir in salt and pepper and take out.
8. Serve and enjoy!

Nutritional Values Per Serving:
Calories: 66; Fat: 2.7g; Carbohydrates: 9.6g; Protein: 3.6g

Ninja Foodi Citrus Carrots

Prep Time: 5 minutes
Cook Time: 5 minutes
Servings: 2

Ingredients:

- 1 tablespoon fresh ginger, minced
- 1 teaspoon olive oil
- ¼ cup fresh orange juice
- 1½ cups carrots, peeled and chopped
- Salt and black pepper, to taste

Directions:
1. Add ginger, carrots and oil in a Ninja Foodi Multi-cooker and press the "Sear" button.
2. Close the pressure Lid and press the "Start/Stop" button.
3. Cook for 2 minutes and open the lid.
4. Add in salt, pepper and orange juice. Stir well.
5. Simmer for about 3 minutes and take out.
6. Serve and enjoy!

Nutritional Values Per Serving:
Calories: 167; Fat: 2.6g; Carbohydrates: 34.9g; Protein: 3g

Gluten-free Taco Beans

Prep Time: 5 Minutes
Cook Time: 20-25 Minutes
Servings: 1

Ingredients:
- ½ cup Albi beans
- 2 cloves minced garlic
- 1 diced onion
- ½ teaspoon of salt and pepper
- 1 tablespoon taco seasoning mix
- 5-7 cups water

Directions:
1. In the pot of Ninja Foodi Multi-Cooker, place your beans, garlic, onions, and the seasonings together.
2. Add water and secure the Ninja Foodi Multi-Cooker Lid and set its valve to Seal.
3. Let it cook for 25 minutes on High Pressure of Ninja Foodi Multi-Cooker setting, but keep in mind if the beans have been soaked already, then cook for 3 minutes only.
4. When the cooking is over do nothing for 10 minutes and let them naturally release and your taco beans are ready!

Nutritional Values Per Serving:
Calories: 126; Fat: 0.5g; Carbohydrates: 20.9g; Protein: 6.6g

Pomegranate Radish Mix

Prep Time: 5 minutes
Cook Time: 8 minutes
Servings: 4

Ingredients:
- 1-pound radishes, roughly cubed
- Black pepper and salt to the taste
- 2 garlic cloves, minced
- ½ cup chicken stock
- 2 tablespoons pomegranate juice
- ¼ cup pomegranate seeds

Directions:
1. In your Ninja Foodi, combine the radishes with the stock and the other ingredients.
2. Put the Ninja Foodi's lid on and cook on High for 8 minutes.
3. Release the pressure quickly for 5 minutes, divide everything between plates and serve.

Nutritional Values Per Serving:
Calories: 133; Fat: 2.3g; Carbohydrates: 2.4g; Protein: 2g

Broccoli Cauliflower

Prep Time: 10 minutes
Cook Time: 15 minutes
Servings: 4

Ingredients:
- 2 cups broccoli florets
- 1 cup cauliflower florets
- 2 tablespoons lime juice
- 1 tablespoon avocado oil
- ⅓ cup tomato sauce
- 2 teaspoons ginger, grated
- 2 teaspoons garlic, minced
- 1 tablespoon chives, chopped

Directions:
1. Set the Foodi on Sauté mode, stir in the oil, heat it up, add the garlic and the ginger and sauté for 2 minutes.
2. Stir in the broccoli, cauliflower and the rest of the ingredients.
3. Put the Ninja Foodi's lid on and cook on High for 13 minutes.
4. naturally Release the pressure for 10 minutes, divide everything between plates and serve.

Nutritional Values Per Serving:
Calories: 118; Fat: 1.5g; Carbohydrates: 4.3g; Protein: 6g

Leeks and Carrots

Prep Time: 5 minutes
Cook Time: 15 minutes
Servings: 4

Ingredients:
- 2 leeks, roughly sliced
- 2 carrots, sliced
- 1 teaspoon ginger powder
- 1 teaspoon garlic powder
- ½ cup chicken stock
- Black pepper and salt to the taste
- 2 tablespoons lemon juice
- 2 tablespoons olive oil
- ½ tablespoon balsamic vinegar

Directions:
1. In your Ninja Foodi, combine the leeks with the carrots and the other ingredients.
2. Put the Ninja Foodi's lid on and cook on High for 15 minutes.
3. Release the pressure quickly for 5 minutes, divide the mix between plates and serve.

Nutritional Values Per Serving:
Calories: 133; Fat: 3.4g; Carbohydrates: 5g; Protein: 2.1g

Vanilla Cheesecake

Prep Time: 15 minutes.
Cook Time: 2 hours
Servings: 6

Ingredients:
For Crust:
- 1 cup almonds, toasted
- 1 egg
- 2 tablespoons butter
- 4-6 drops liquid stevia

For Filling:
- 2 8-ounce packages of cream cheese, softened
- 4 tablespoons heavy cream
- 2 eggs
- 1 tablespoon coconut flour
- 1 teaspoon liquid stevia
- 1 teaspoon vanilla extract

Directions:
1. For the crust: in a high-speed food processor, stir in almonds and pulse until a flour-like consistency is achieved.
2. In a suitable, add ground almond, egg, butter and stevia and mix until well combined.
3. In the bottom of a 1½-quart oval pan, place the crust mixture and press to smooth the top surface, leaving a little room on each side.
4. For the filling: in a suitable, stir in all ingredients and with an immersion blender, blend until well combined.
5. Place the prepared filling mixture over the crust evenly.
6. In the Ninja Foodi's insert, place 1 cup of water.
7. Carefully set the pan in the Ninja Foodi's insert.
8. Close the Ninja Foodi's lid with a pressure lid and select "Slow Cook".
9. Set on "Low" for 2 hours.
10. Press the "Start/Stop" button to initiate cooking.
11. Place the pan onto a wire rack to cool.
12. Refrigerate to chill for at least 6-8 hours before serving.

Nutritional Values Per Serving:
Calories: 446; Fats: 42.9g; Carbohydrates: 7.2g; Proteins: 10.6g

Yogurt Cheesecake

Prep Time: 10 minutes.
Cook Time: 40 minutes
Servings: 8

Ingredients:
- 4 cups plain Greek Yogurt
- 1 cup Erythritol
- ½ teaspoon vanilla extract

Directions:
1. Line a cake pans with Parchment paper.
2. In a suitable, stir in the yogurt and Erythritol and with a hand mixer, mix well.
3. Stir in vanilla extract and mix to combine.
4. Add the mixture into the prepared pan and cover with a paper kitchen towel.
5. Then with a piece of foil, cover the pan tightly.
6. In the Ninja Foodi's insert, place 1 cup of water.
7. Set a "Reversible Rack" in the Ninja Foodi's insert.
8. Place the ramekins over the "Reversible Rack".
9. Close the Ninja Foodi's lid with a pressure lid and place the pressure valve to the "Seal" position.
10. Select "Pressure" mode and set it to "High" for 40 minutes.
11. Press the "Start/Stop" button to initiate cooking.
12. Switch the pressure valve to "Vent" and do a "Quick" release.
13. Place the pan onto a wire rack and remove the foil and paper towel.
14. Again, cover the pan with a new paper towel and refrigerate to cool overnight.

Nutritional Values Per Serving:
Calories: 88; Fats: 1.5g; Carbohydrates: 8.7g; Proteins: 7g

Chocolate Cheesecake

Prep Time: 15 minutes.
Cook Time: 20 minutes
Servings: 10

Ingredients:
For Crust
- ¼ cup coconut flour
- ¼ cup almond flour
- 2½ tablespoons cacao powder
- 1½ tablespoons Erythritol
- 2 tablespoons butter, melted

For Filling
- 16 ounces cream cheese, softened
- ⅓ cup cacao powder
- ½ teaspoon powdered Erythritol
- ½ teaspoon stevia powder
- 1 large egg
- 2 large egg yolks
- 6 ounces unsweetened dark chocolate, melted
- ¾ cup heavy cream
- ¼ cup sour cream
- 1 teaspoon vanilla extract

Directions:
1. For the crust: in a suitable, mix together flours, cacao powder and Erythritol.
2. Stir in the melted butter and mix until well combined.
3. Stir in the mixture into a parchment paper-lined 7-inch springform pan evenly, and with your fingers, press evenly.
4. For filling: in a food processor, add the cream cheese, cacao powder, monk fruit powder and stevia and pulse until smooth.
5. Stir in the egg and egg yolks and pulse until well combined.
6. Add the rest of the ingredients and pulse until well combined.
7. Place the prepared filling mixture on top of the crust evenly and with a rubber spatula, smooth the surface.
8. With a piece of foil, cover the springform pan loosely.
9. In the Ninja Foodi's insert, place 2 cups of water.
10. Set a "Reversible Rack" in the Ninja Foodi's insert.
11. Place the springform pan over the "Reversible Rack".
12. Close the Ninja Foodi's lid with a pressure lid and place the pressure valve in the "Seal" position.
13. Select "Pressure" mode and set it to "High" for 20 minutes.
14. Press the "Start/Stop" button to initiate cooking.
15. Switch the pressure valve to "Vent" and do a "Natural" release.
16. Place the pan onto a wire rack to cool completely.
17. Refrigerate for about 6-8 hours before serving.

Nutritional Values Per Serving:
Calories: 385; Fats: 35.6g; Carbohydrates: 9.8g; Proteins: 8.9g

Mini Chocolate Cheesecakes

Prep Time: 15 minutes.
Cook Time: 18 minutes
Servings: 4

Ingredients:
- 1 egg
- 8 ounces cream cheese, softened
- ¼ cup Erythritol
- 1 tablespoon powdered peanut butter
- ¾ tablespoon cacao powder

Directions:
1. Grease the Ninja Foodi's insert.
2. In a blender, stir in the eggs and cream cheese and pulse until smooth.
3. Add the rest of the ingredients and pulse until well combined.
4. Transfer the mixture into 2 8-ounce mason jars evenly.
5. In the Ninja Foodi's insert, place 1 cup of water.
6. Set a "Reversible Rack" in the Ninja Foodi's insert.
7. Place the mason jars over the "Reversible Rack".
8. Close the Ninja Foodi's lid with a pressure lid and place the pressure valve in the "Seal" position.
9. Select "Pressure" mode and set it to "High" for 18 minutes.
10. Press the "Start/Stop" button to initiate cooking.
11. Switch the pressure valve to "Vent" and do a "Natural" release.
12. Open the Ninja Foodi's lid and place the ramekins onto a wire rack to cool.
13. Refrigerate to chill for at least 6-8 hours before serving.

Nutritional Values Per Serving:
Calories: 222; Fats: 28.4g; Carbohydrates: 2.9g; Proteins: 6.5g

Lime Blueberry Cheesecake

Prep Time: 15 minutes.
Cook Time: 30 minutes
Servings: 6

Ingredients:
- ¼ cup 1 teaspoon Erythritol
- 8 ounces cream cheese, softened
- ⅓ cup Ricotta cheese
- 1 teaspoon fresh lime zest, grated
- 2 tablespoons fresh lime juice
- ½ teaspoon vanilla extract
- 1 cup blueberries
- 2 eggs
- 2 tablespoons sour cream

Directions:
1. In a suitable, stir in ¼ cup of Erythritol and remaining ingredients except for eggs and sour cream and with a hand mixer, beat on high speed until smooth.
2. Stir in the eggs and beat on low speed until well combined, then fold in blueberries.
3. Transfer the mixture into a 6-inch greased springform pan evenly.
4. With a piece of foil, cover the pan.
5. In the Ninja Foodi's insert, place 2 cups of water.
6. Set a "Reversible Rack" in the Ninja Foodi's insert.
7. Place the springform pan over the "Reversible Rack".
8. Close the Ninja Foodi's lid with a pressure lid and place the pressure valve in the "Seal" position.
9. Select "Pressure" mode and set it to "High" for 30 minutes.
10. Press the "Start/Stop" button to initiate cooking.
11. Switch the pressure valve to "Vent" and do a "Natural" release.
12. Place the pan onto a wire rack to cool slightly.
13. Meanwhile, in a small bowl, stir in the sour cream and remaining erythritol and beat until well combined.

14. Spread the cream mixture on the warm cake evenly.
15. Refrigerate for about 6-8 hours before serving.

Nutritional Values Per Serving:
Calories: 182; Fats: 16.6g; Carbohydrates: 2.1g; Proteins: 6.4g

Chocolate Walnut Cake

Prep Time: 15 minutes.
Cook Time: 20 minutes
Servings: 6

Ingredients:
- 3 eggs
- 1 cup almond flour
- ⅔ cup Erythritol
- ⅓ cup heavy whipping cream
- ¼ cup butter softened
- ¼ cup cacao powder
- ¼ cup walnuts, chopped
- 1 teaspoon baking powder

Directions:
1. In a suitable bowl, mix all the ingredients and with a mixer, beat until fluffy.
2. Add the mixture into a greased Bundt pan.
3. With a piece of foil, cover the pan.
4. In the Ninja Foodi's insert, place 2 cups of water.
5. Set a "Reversible Rack" in the Ninja Foodi's insert.
6. Place the Bundt pan over the "Reversible Rack".
7. Close the Ninja Foodi's lid with a pressure lid and place the pressure valve to the "Seal" position.
8. Select "Pressure" mode and set it to "High" for 20 minutes.
9. Press the "Start/Stop" button to initiate cooking.
10. Switch the pressure valve to "Vent" and do a "Quick" release.
11. Place the pan onto a wire rack to cool for about 10 minutes.
12. Flip the baked and cooled cake onto the wire rack to cool completely.
13. Cut into desired-sized slices and serve.

Nutritional Values Per Serving:
Calories: 270; Fats: 25.4g; Carbohydrates: 7g; Proteins: 8.9g

Ninja Foodi Vanilla Shake

Prep Time: 7 minutes
Cook Time: 2 minutes
Servings: 2

Ingredients:
- 1 cup water
- 1 cup almond milk
- ½ cup vanilla ice cream
- 2 teaspoons sugar

Directions:
1. Add every ingredient in the Ninja Foodi Multi-cooker and select "Pressure".
2. Close the pressure Lid and press the "Start/Stop'" button.
3. Cook for 2 minutes and open the lid.
4. Take out and set aside.
5. Refrigerate overnight, serve and enjoy!

Nutritional Values Per Serving:
Calories: 325; Fat: 30.4g; Carbohydrates: 14.7g; Protein: 3.3g

Ninja Foodi Mocha Cake

Prep Time: 2 minutes
Cook Time: 2 minutes
Servings: 4

Ingredients:
- ½ cup water
- 2 tablespoons beaten egg
- 4 teaspoons chocolate chips
- ½ teaspoon baking powder
- 4 teaspoons Splenda
- 4 teaspoons coffee

Directions:
1. Add all the ingredients to a large bowl and mix well.
2. Place the bowl in Ninja Foodi Multi-cooker, press the "Bake" button and close the lid.
3. Press the "Start/Stop" button and bake for 2 minutes.
4. Open the lid and take out.
5. Serve and enjoy!

Nutritional Values Per Serving:
Calories: 46; Fat: 1.5g; Carbohydrates: 6.4g; Protein: 0.8g

Ninja Foodi Chia Seed Smoothie

Prep Time: 10 minutes
Cook Time: 2 minutes
Servings: 2

Ingredients:
- 2 cups unsweetened almond milk
- ½ cup chia seeds
- 2 teaspoons sugar

Directions:
1. Add almond milk, chia seeds and sugar in a Ninja Foodi Multi-cooker and select "Pressure".
2. Close the pressure lid and press the "Start/Stop" button.
3. Cook for 2 minutes and open the lid.
4. Take out and refrigerate overnight.
5. Serve and enjoy!

Nutritional Values Per Serving:
Calories: 89; Fat: 5.7g; Carbohydrates: 9g; Protein: 2.2g

Ninja Foodi Fruity Frozen Treat

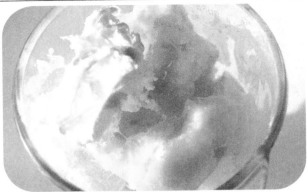

Prep Time: 5 minutes
Cook Time: 3 minutes
Servings: 3

Ingredients:
- ½ cup frozen pineapple chunks
- 1 cup almond milk
- 4 tablespoons fresh lime juice
- 2 cups banana slices

Directions:
1. Add pineapple slices, almond milk, lime juice and banana slices in a Ninja Foodi Multi-cooker and select "Pressure".
2. Close the pressure Lid and press the "Start/Stop" button.
3. Cook for about 3 minutes and open the lid.
4. Dish out and freeze for about 1 hour.
5. Take out, serve and enjoy!

Nutritional Values Per Serving:
Calories: 464; Fat: 31.4g; Carbohydrates: 45.2g; Protein: 5.4g

Ninja Foodi Ricotta Mousse

Prep Time: 10 minutes
Cook Time: 2 minutes
Servings: 2

Ingredients:
- 2½ cups water
- 2 teaspoons stevia powder
- ½ teaspoon vanilla extract
- 1 cup ricotta cheese
- 2 teaspoons cocoa powder

Directions:
1. Add everything to a Ninja Foodi Multi-cooker and select "pressure".
2. Close the pressure Lid and press the "Start/Stop" button.
3. Cook for about 2 minutes and open the lid.
4. Pour the mixture in serving glasses and refrigerate for about 6 hours.
5. Serve and enjoy!

Nutritional Values Per Serving:
Calories: 178; Fat: 10.1g; Carbohydrates: 7.5g; Protein: 14.5g

Ninja Foodi Chickpea Fudge

Prep Time: 10 minutes
Cook Time: 1 hour 5 minutes
Servings: 3

Ingredients:
- ½ cup cooked chickpeas
- 2 dates, pitted and chopped
- ½ tablespoon cocoa powder
- 2 tablespoons almond butter
- 2 tablespoons almond milk
- ¼ teaspoon vanilla extract

Directions:
1. Add everything except cocoa powder in the Ninja Foodi Multi-cooker and select "Pressure".
2. Close thepressure Lid and press the "Start/Stop" button.
3. Cook for about 5 minutes and open the lid.
4. Transfer the mixture to a bowl and stir in cocoa powder.
5. Pour the mixture in Ninja Foodi Multi-cooker and press the "Bake" button.
6. Bake for about an hour and take out.
7. Refrigerate, slice and serve.

Nutritional Values Per Serving:
Calories: 228; Fat: 10.5g; Carbohydrates: 27.4g; Protein: 9.2g

Ninja Foodi Blackberry Crumble

Prep Time: 10 minutes
Cook Time: 45 minutes
Servings: 6

Ingredients:
Blackberries Filling:
- ¼ cup coconut flour
- 3 tablespoons water
- ¼ cup arrowroot flour
- 2 tablespoons melted butter
- ¼ cup mashed banana
- 1½ cups fresh blackberries
- ¾ teaspoon baking soda
- ½ tablespoon lemon juice

Crumble Topping
- ½ cup old fashioned oats
- ½ cup coconut flour
- ½ cup brown sugar, packed
- ⅛ tsp baking powder
- ⅛ tsp baking soda
- ¼ cup butter, softened

Directions:
1. Add all the ingredients for filling except blackberries in a bowl and mix well.
2. Combine the ingredients for crumble topping in another bowl.
3. Arrange blackberries in the bottom of Ninja Foodi Multi-cooker and pour the filling batter on them.
4. Top with the crumble topping.
5. Press the "Bake" button and close the lid.
6. Press the "Start/Stop" button and bake for 40 minutes at 300 degrees F.
7. Open the lid and take out.
8. Serve and enjoy!

Nutritional Values Per Serving:
Calories: 292; Fat: 10.7g; Carbohydrates: 45.7g; Protein: 5.9g

Ninja Foodi Yogurt Cheesecake

Prep Time: 15 minutes
Cook Time: 30 minutes
Servings: 10

Ingredients:
- 6 drops liquid stevia
- 1 teaspoon vanilla extract
- 4 egg whites
- ½ cup cocoa powder
- 3 cups low-fat Greek yogurt
- ¼ cup arrowroot starch
- Pinch of salt
Crust
- ¼ cup white sugar
- 7 graham crackers
- ¼ cup brown sugar
- 1 pinch salt
- 6 tablespoons butter, melted

Directions:
1. Gather all the crust ingredients and dump into the blender.
2. Blend until all the ingredients are well combined and form the sand like consistency.
3. Combine all crust ingredients in a blender and blend until mixture becomes the consistency of damp sand.
4. Shift the crust mixture into a 7-inch springform pan and pat it down with spatula.
5. Add all the ingredients of cheesecake filling in a large bowl and mix well.
6. Pour the mixture in the springform pan over the top of the crust and place it in the pot of Ninja Foodi Multi-cooker.
7. Press the "Bake" button and close the Crisping Lid.
8. Press the "Start/Stop" button and bake for about 30 minutes at 350 degrees F.
9. Open the lid and take out.
10. Slice and serve.

Nutritional Values Per Serving:
Calories: 236; Fat: 9.3g; Carbohydrates: 35.1g; Protein: 5.9g

Ninja Foodi Banana Custard

Prep Time: 10 minutes
Cook Time: 25 minutes
Servings: 4

Ingredients:
- 1 banana, mashed
- 1 cup almond milk
- ¼ teaspoon vanilla extract
- 2 eggs

Directions:
1. Add all the ingredients in a large bowl and mix well.
2. Pour the batter evenly in custard cups and place them in Ninja Foodi Multi-cooker.
3. Press the "Bake" button and close the Crisping Lid.
4. Press the "Start/Stop" button and bake for 25 minutes at 350 degrees F.
5. Open the lid and take out.
6. Serve and enjoy!

Nutritional Values Per Serving:
Calories: 196; Fat: 16.6g; Carbohydrates: 10.3g; Protein: 4.5g

Ninja Foodi Chocolate Tofu Mousse

Prep Time: 10 minutes
Cook Time: 1 minute
Servings: 2

Ingredients:
- 1 banana, peeled and sliced
- ¾ cup firm tofu, drained
- 1 teaspoon cocoa powder
- 1 teaspoon chopped almonds

Directions:
1. Add all the ingredients in a Ninja Foodi Multi-cooker and select "Pressure".
2. Close the lid and press the "Start/Stop" button.
3. Cook for 1 minute and open the lid.
4. Pour the mixture in serving glasses and refrigerate for about 3 hours.
5. Take out, serve and enjoy!

Nutritional Values Per Serving:
Calories: 264; Fat: 2.7g; Carbohydrates: 51.7g; Protein: 14.2g

Ninja Foodi Raspberry Ice Cream

Prep Time: 20 minutes
Cook Time: 2 minutes
Servings: 4

Ingredients:
- 1 cup fresh raspberries
- ½ banana, sliced
- 2 tablespoons shredded coconut
- ½ cup coconut cream

Directions:
1. Add all the ingredients in a Ninja Foodi Multi-cooker and select "Pressure".
2. Close the lid, press the "Start/Stop" button and cook for about 2 minutes.
3. Open the lid and transfer the mixture to an ice-cream maker.
4. Process according to manufacturer's directions and take out.
5. Pour the mixture into an air-tight container and freeze for about 4 hours. Stir after every half an hour.
6. Take out and serve.

Nutritional Values Per Serving:
Calories: 107; Fat: 8.2g; Carbohydrates: 9.1g; Protein: 1.3g

Rocky Road Fudge

Prep Time: 5 Minutes
Cook Time: 5 hours
Servings: 6

Ingredients:
- 8 ounces pretend condensed milk
- 9 ounces chocolate chips
- 1 teaspoon vanilla extract
- ¼ teaspoon sea salt
- ½ cup almonds
- 2 ounces marshmallows

Directions:
1. On Broil, preheat the Ninja Foodi Multi-Cooker for 10 minutes with the Basket inside. Now add almonds to the Basket and Broil it for 3 to 5 minutes. Take out the almonds and let them cool.
2. Line the square pan with parchment paper, add in chocolate chips and sweetened condensed milk, and then cover it again with the foil.
3. Place the pan in Ninja Foodi Multi-Cooker. Add two cups of water in it and cook at Steam setting for 5 minutes.
4. Set the valve to the Vent position while the chocolate mixture is steaming.
5. Meanwhile, crush the almonds coarsely and cut marshmallows if you're using large ones.
6. Remove the pan from Ninja Foodi Multi-Cooker and add vanilla, marshmallows, salt, and chopped almonds. Give it a good mix.
7. Then the fudge will start to thicken up as it cools down. Let it cool down for two to four hours in the refrigerator and cut it into bite-size squares!

Nutritional Values Per Serving:
Calories: 328; Fat: 18.7g; Carbohydrates: 38.1g; Protein: 7.1g

Biscuit Donuts

Prep Time: 5 Minutes
Cook Time: 8-10 Minutes
Servings: 8

Ingredients:
- 16 ounces flaky layers biscuits
- ½ cup butter unsalted
- ¼ cup brown sugar
- ½ cup sugar
- 1 teaspoon grounded cinnamon
- ¼ teaspoon salt

Directions:
1. Take sugar, brown sugar, cinnamon, and salt in a small bowl and mix well to combine the ingredients.
2. Now, on a flat surface, align the flaky biscuits. Take a clean bottle cap and press it in the center of the biscuit creating the hole of the donuts.
3. Spray the Ninja Foodi Multi-Cooker Cook & Crisp Basket with olive oil. Place four donuts in the Basket of the Ninja Foodi Multi-Cooker and close the lid. Press the option Start/Stop then Air Crisp it at 390° F for about 10 minutes then press the Start/Stop button again. Keep in mind to check a couple of times to make sure they don't overbake.
4. Open the Ninja Foodi Multi-Cooker after 10 minutes and take out your fresh donuts.
5. The second batch of donuts usually takes 7 to 8 minutes for Bake.
6. Drench the donuts one at a time in the melted butter once all the donuts are air-fried.
7. Then invert them into the dry ingredients to coat them generously.
8. Repeat this process until all donuts are coated, enjoy them warm and appropriately store the leftovers!

Nutritional Values Per Serving:
Calories: 341; Fat: 16.8g; Carbohydrates: 34.3g; Protein: 3.3g

Pineapple Chunks

Prep Time: 3 Minutes
Cook Time: 10-12 Minutes
Servings: 6

Ingredients:
- 1 stick melted butter
- ½ cup brown sugar
- ½ teaspoon cinnamon
- 1 sliced pineapple

Directions:
1. Combine melted butter, cinnamon, and brown sugar in a low-sided dish. Mix it well.
2. Put in your pineapple pieces to allow it to soak in the flavors for a bit.
3. Select the Bake option, and set the temperature to 375° F. Add pineapple pieces and let them Bake for 12 minutes.
4. Flip the pineapple slices gently halfway through.
5. Serve immediately when ready!

Nutritional Values Per Serving:
Calories: 455; Fat: 22.4g; Carbohydrates: 39g; Protein: 4.5g

Banana Bread

Prep Time: 10 Minutes
Cook Time: 30 Minutes
Servings: 4

Ingredients
- 2 large ripe bananas
- ¾ cup all-purpose flour
- 1 egg
- 3 teaspoons brown sugar
- 2 teaspoons butter
- ¼ cup sour cream
- ½ teaspoon baking soda
- ½ teaspoon salt

Directions:
1. Preheat the Ninja Foodi Multi-Cooker at Bake Mode at 375° F.
2. Now grease the mini loaf and set it aside.
3. Take all ingredients in a medium bowl and combine them and stir until combined well.
4. Put the batter evenly in a butter paper-lined loaf pan. Dump the pan and Bake it for 25 to 30 minutes.
5. To check the doneness, make sure that when a toothpick is inserted in the center, it comes out clean. Check the banana bread with a toothpick and serve it warm!

Nutritional Values Per Serving:
Calories: 271; Fat: 10.4g; Carbohydrates: 40.8g; Protein: 4.8g

Honey Almond Scones

Prep Time: 5 Minutes
Cook Time: 6 Minutes
Servings: 6

Ingredients:
- 2 cups all-purpose flour
- 3 tablespoons brown sugar
- 1 egg
- 1 teaspoon baking powder
- ½ teaspoon salt
- 1 cup milk
- 1 teaspoon almond extract
- ¼ cup butter
- Cinnamon to sprinkle

Directions:
1. Combine the dried ingredients in a large bowl. Melt butter in a pan, then adds it to dry ingredients.
2. Now combine all the wet ingredients with the dry ones and stir it. Make sure to not overwork with the dough mixture.
3. Place on parchment paper in Ninja Foodi Multi-Cooker Cook & Crisp Basket. Scoop out the dough with a rounded spoon on the Ninja Foodi Multi-Cooker Basket. Set your Ninja Foodi Multi-Cooker to an Air Crisp function and

set the temperature at 390° F for 8 minutes until it's golden brown.
4. Let the cones cool down and then sprinkle a little bit of cinnamon!

Nutritional Values Per Serving:
Calories: 267; Fat: 9.9g; Carbohydrates: 37.4g; Protein: 6.5g

Chocolate Chip Cookies

Prep Time: 4 Minutes
Cook Time: 10 Minutes
Servings: 8

Ingredients:
- ½ cup butter
- ½ cup sugar
- 1 egg
- 1 teaspoon vanilla essence
- ¼ cup light brown sugar
- ½ teaspoon baking soda
- ¼ teaspoon salt
- ¾ cup all-purpose flour
- 1 cup chocolate chips or chocolate chunks

Directions:
1. Preheat the Ninja Foodi Multi-Cooker at Air Crisp Mode at 390° F then grease a metal cookie pan that fits the Ninja Foodi Multi-Cooker. You can use the cookie cutter and place it in a baking tray.
2. Combine butter, brown sugar, and sugar, and cream.
3. Now add vanilla essence and egg. Mix it well until combined.
4. Add in baking soda, flour, and salt. Now stir in chocolate chips. Give it a good mix.
5. Flatten the cookie dough and press it in the bottom of the greased pan. Dump it in the Ninja Foodi Multi-Cooker and bake for ten to 12 minutes until it becomes slightly brown around the edges!

Nutritional Values Per Serving:
Calories: 364; Fat: 20.3g; Carbohydrates: 42.8g; Protein: 4g

Mini Vanilla Cheesecakes

Prep Time: 15 minutes.
Cook Time: 10 minutes
Servings: 4

Ingredients:
- ¾ cup Erythritol
- 2 eggs
- 1 teaspoon vanilla extract
- ½ teaspoon fresh lemon juice
- 16 ounces cream cheese, softened
- 2 tablespoon sour cream

Directions:
1. Set the "Air Crisp Basket" in the Ninja Foodi's insert.
2. Close the Ninja Foodi's lid with a crisping lid and select "Air Crisp".
3. Set its cooking temperature to 350 degrees F for 5 minutes.
4. Press the "Start/Stop" button to initiate preheating.
5. In a blender, stir in the Erythritol, eggs, vanilla extract and lemon juice and pulse until smooth.
6. Stir in the cream cheese along with sour cream and pulse until smooth.
7. Stir in the mixture into 2- 4-inch spring-form pans evenly.
8. After preheating, Open the Ninja Foodi's lid.
9. Place the pans into the "Air Crisp Basket".
10. Close the Ninja Foodi's lid with a crisping lid and select "Air Crisp".
11. Set its cooking temperature to 350 degrees for 10 minutes.
12. Press the "Start/Stop" button to initiate cooking.
13. Place the pans onto a wire rack for 10 minutes.
14. Refrigerator overnight before serving.

Nutritional Values Per Serving:
Calories: 436; Fats: 21g; Carbohydrates: 3.2g; Proteins: 13.1g

4 Weeks Meal Plan

Week 1

Day 1
Breakfast: Ninja Foodi Ham Muffins
Lunch: Radish Apples Salad
Dinner: Ninja Foodi Carrot & Pork Stew
Snack: Ninja Foodi Popcorn
Dessert: Yogurt Cheesecake

Day 2
Breakfast: Nutmeg Pumpkin Porridge
Lunch: Hawaiian Fried Rice
Dinner: Panko Crusted Cod
Snack: Glazed Walnuts
Dessert: Chocolate Cheesecake

Day 3
Breakfast: Apricot Oatmeal
Lunch: Veggie Pot Pie
Dinner: Ninja Foodi Squid Rings
Snack: Chicken Pork Nuggets
Dessert: Mini Chocolate Cheesecakes

Day 4
Breakfast: Swiss Bacon Frittata
Lunch: Air Crisped Brussels Sprouts
Dinner: Ninja Foodi Duck Stew
Snack: Garlicky Tomato
Dessert: Ninja Foodi Vanilla Shake

Day 5
Breakfast: Ham Breakfast Casserole
Lunch: Ninja Foodi Asparagus Soup
Dinner: Ninja Foodi Plum & Beef Salad
Snack: Jalapeno Salsa
Dessert: Chocolate Walnut Cake

Day 6
Breakfast: Deviled Eggs
Lunch: Ninja Foodi Vegetables Smoothie
Dinner: Ninja Foodi Salmon
Snack: Ninja Foodi Spicy Popcorns
Dessert: Ninja Foodi Chia Seed Smoothie

Day 7
Breakfast: Ninja Foodi Coconut Cereal
Lunch: Ninja Foodi Broccoli Soup
Dinner: Carne Guisada
Snack: Ninja Foodi Cod Sticks
Dessert: Ninja Foodi Chickpea Fudge

Week 2

Day 1
Breakfast: Ninja Foodi Baked Eggs
Lunch: Pomegranate Radish Mix
Dinner: Ninja Foodi Chicken & Carrot Stew
Snack: Cauliflower Nuggets
Dessert: Ninja Foodi Ricotta Mousse

Day 2
Breakfast: Brussels Sprouts Bacon Hash
Lunch: Cauliflower chunks with Lemon Sauce
Dinner: Ninja Foodi Lamb & Kale Stew
Snack: Crispy Onion Rings
Dessert: Ninja Foodi Fruity Frozen Treat

Day 3
Breakfast: Chicken Omelet
Lunch: Balsamic Cabbage with Endives
Dinner: Ninja Foodi Parsley Baked Salmon
Snack: Japanese Eggs
Dessert: Lime Blueberry Cheesecake

Day 4
Breakfast: Vanilla Banana Bread
Lunch: Maple Dipped Kale
Dinner: Beef Sirloin Steak
Snack: Shallots with Mushrooms
Dessert: Vanilla Cheesecake

Day 5
Breakfast: Almond Quinoa Porridge
Lunch: Ninja Foodi Spinach and Onion Soup
Dinner: Ninja Foodi Salmon Soup
Snack: Crispy Chicken Skin
Dessert: Ninja Foodi Mocha Cake

Day 6
Breakfast: Chorizo Omelet
Lunch: Cabbage with Bacon
Dinner: Ninja Foodi Ground Turkey
Snack: Ninja Foodi Spinach Chips
Dessert: Ninja Foodi Blackberry Crumble

Day 7
Breakfast: Pepperoni Omelets
Lunch: Cabbage with Carrots
Dinner: Ninja Foodi Steak Fajitas
Snack: Ninja Foodi Cheddar Biscuits
Dessert: Ninja Foodi Yogurt Cheesecake

Week 3

Day 1
Breakfast: Ninja Foodi Eggs with Spinach
Lunch: Saucy Kale
Dinner: Ninja Foodi Stir-Fried Shrimp
Snack: Ninja Foodi Spiced Almonds
Dessert: Ninja Foodi Banana Custard

Day 2
Breakfast: Hashbrown Casserole
Lunch: Ninja Foodi Tomato Olive Salad
Dinner: Ninja Foodi Lamb & Carrot Stew
Snack: Shallot Pepper Pancakes
Dessert: Ninja Foodi Raspberry Ice Cream

Day 3
Breakfast: Breakfast pizza
Lunch: Ninja Foodi Kale Salad
Dinner: Chicken Tortilla
Snack: Ninja Foodi Banana Cookies
Dessert: Biscuit Donuts

Day 4
Breakfast: Ninja Foodi Arugula Omelet
Lunch: Beets and Carrots
Dinner: Char Siu Pork
Snack: Ninja Foodi Spicy Cashews
Dessert: Banana Bread

Day 5
Breakfast: Breakfast Oats Bowl
Lunch: Sesame Radish
Dinner: Ninja Foodi Broiled Mahi-Mahi
Snack: Garlic Pretzels with Ranch Dressing
Dessert: Chocolate Chip Cookies

Day 6
Breakfast: Ninja Foodi Hard-boiled eggs
Lunch: Ninja Foodi Vegetable Curry
Dinner: Mixed Seafood Platter
Snack: Ninja Foodi Herb Crackers
Dessert: Yogurt Cheesecake

Day 7
Breakfast: Egg rolls
Lunch: Ninja Foodi Citrus Carrots
Dinner: Ninja Foodi Chicken & Salsa Chili
Snack: Ninja Foodi Lemon Scones
Dessert: Chocolate Walnut Cake

Week 4

Day 1
Breakfast: Avocado Cups
Lunch: Bell Peppers Mix
Dinner: Ninja Foodi Duck Fajita Platter
Snack: Zucchini Egg Tots
Dessert: Ninja Foodi Chocolate Tofu Mousse

Day 2
Breakfast: Ninja Foodi Cinnamon Tea
Lunch: Ninja Foodi Roasted Red Pepper Gazpacho
Dinner: Ninja Foodi Beef Casserole
Snack: Ninja Foodi Spicy Peanuts
Dessert: Rocky Road Fudge

Day 3
Breakfast: Ninja Foodi Broccoli Pancakes
Lunch: Minty Radishes
Dinner: Ninja Foodi Spinach Chicken
Snack: Ninja Foodi Chickpea Crackers
Dessert: Pineapple Chunks

Day 4
Breakfast: Ninja Foodi Pancakes
Lunch: Steak and Veggie Bowl
Dinner: Ninja Foodi Air Crisp Herbed Salmon
Snack: Chicken Wings
Dessert: Honey Almond Scones

Day 5
Breakfast: Fruit Pancakes
Lunch: Kale and Parmesan
Dinner: Salmon Kale Meal
Snack: Buffalo Cauliflower Platter
Dessert: Mini Vanilla Cheesecakes

Day 6
Breakfast: French Toast Bites
Lunch: Carrots Walnuts Salad
Dinner: Ninja Foodi Cranberry Chicken
Snack: Air Crisped Chicken Nuggets
Dessert: Mini Chocolate Cheesecakes

Day 7
Breakfast: Nutmeg Pumpkin Porridge
Lunch: Gluten-free Taco Beans
Dinner: Maple Glazed Pork Chops
Snack: Coated Onion Rings
Dessert: Ninja Foodi Vanilla Shake

Conclusion

The Ninja Foodi Multi-Cooker is a one-of-a-kind cooking appliance. It takes the place of your Pressure Cook, Air Crisp, and slow cooker. In one compact kitchen machine, you can steam, bake, roast, pressure cook, air-fry, and slow cook. To make flavorful, multi-textured meals in one pot, cook proteins, grains, and your favorite vegetables all at the same time. Air-Fry is a healthier way to enjoy fried favorites, that uses little to no oil. Traditional frying methods use up to 75% less fat. Ninja Foodi Multi-Cooker is very easy to handle machine which have specific buttons to control all its setting to cook food accordingly. So, you can quickly and easily create delicious meals, sides, snacks, and desserts with the Ninja Foodi Multi-Cooker.

Appendix Measurement Conversion Chart

VOLUME EQUIVALENTS(DRY)

US STANDARD	METRIC (APPROXIMATE)
1/8 teaspoon	0.5 mL
1/4 teaspoon	1 mL
1/2 teaspoon	2 mL
3/4 teaspoon	4 mL
1 teaspoon	5 mL
1 tablespoon	15 mL
1/4 cup	59 mL
1/2 cup	118 mL
3/4 cup	177 mL
1 cup	235 mL
2 cups	475 mL
3 cups	700 mL
4 cups	1 L

WEIGHT EQUIVALENTS

US STANDARD	METRIC (APPROXIMATE)
1 ounce	28 g
2 ounces	57 g
5 ounces	142 g
10 ounces	284 g
15 ounces	425 g
16 ounces (1 pound)	455 g
1.5 pounds	680 g
2 pounds	907 g

VOLUME EQUIVALENTS(LIQUID)

US STANDARD	US STANDARD (OUNCES)	METRIC (APPROXIMATE)
2 tablespoons	1 fl.oz.	30 mL
1/4 cup	2 fl.oz.	60 mL
1/2 cup	4 fl.oz.	120 mL
1 cup	8 fl.oz.	240 mL
1 1/2 cup	12 fl.oz.	355 mL
2 cups or 1 pint	16 fl.oz.	475 mL
4 cups or 1 quart	32 fl.oz.	1 L
1 gallon	128 fl.oz.	4 L

TEMPERATURES EQUIVALENTS

FAHRENHEIT(F)	CELSIUS(C) (APPROXIMATE)
225 °F	107 °C
250 °F	120 °C
275 °F	135 °C
300 °F	150 °C
325 °F	160 °C
350 °F	180 °C
375 °F	190 °C
400 °F	205 °C
425 °F	220 °C
450 °F	235 °C
475 °F	245 °C
500 °F	260 °C

Printed in Great Britain
by Amazon